PRAYER RAIN

An Essential Master-key
for Christian Pilgrims
for Retreat & The Holy Land

Isaac O. Ajibolorunrin

Grosvenor House
Publishing Limited

This book is published by
Grosvenor House Publishing Ltd
Link House
140 The Broadway, Tolworth, Surrey, KT6 7HT.
www.grosvenorhousepublishing.co.uk

A CIP record for this book
is available from the British Library

ISBN 978-1-80381-646-3

King James Version

Scripture taken from Authorized (King James) Version (AKJV) KJV
reproduced by permission of Cambridge University Press,
the Crown's patentee in UK.

New King James Version

Scripture taken from the New King James Version®.
Copyright © 1982 by Thomas Nelson. Used by permission.
All rights reserved. Unless otherwise stated, all Bible passages
quoted in this book are from New King James Version, (NKJV).

The Living Bible

The Living Bible. Verses marked TLB are taken from
The Living Bible, copyright © 1971. Used by permission of
Tyndale House Publishers, Inc., Wheaton, Illinois 60189.
All rights reserved.

DEDICATION

This book is dedicated to Amnon Betsser (aka Papa)

CONTENTS

ACKNOWLEDGEMENTS

A posthumous special thanks to Amnon Betsser. He was a devoted Tour Guide in The Holy Land for over fifty years before he went to be with the Lord on 01/02/2022. I used to call him the Professor of all Tour Guides I have ever known and patronised so far. Most people will remember him through his popular song—*My Sunshine*. For me, he was more than a Tour Guide because my relationship with him grew to the level of a true friend, a genuine 'uncle' and a part of my family who always took upon himself the responsibility for my personal welfare whether on my personal pilgrimage to Israel, or group pilgrimage.

We were so close that even the little details about my food became one of his top priorities. He would take care of everything. He was aware I would not eat any bread and he knew the Bakery to get my special bread from. Believe it or not, he would place the order for my type of bread and ensure it was available and meet me with it on my arrival at the airport. When it is time to return to UK, we would get to the airport early and spend some more time together, he would insist that I take extra money (US Dollars) from him in case I decide to buy some duty-free goods after we have parted, and would say to me, 'refund me when you come back next time,' then bid each other farewell. Bless him.

He would call me any time to check in on me whether in London or Africa. He was so caring that even the Sunday (30/01/2022) preceding his passing to glory he called me during my Church Service, unfortunately that was the last call to me while alive. Anyone who knew him would testify that he was passionate about his job, caring, loving and pastoral to all his clients. You need something? Just ask Papa, and consider it done. His services to all his clients was unique and first class—always. Adieu Papa, adieu my friend and uncle.

Most especially, I am grateful to God for everything He has done for me, my family and ministry and all He continues to do for us.

PREFACE

I decided to write this Prayer book for Christians and believers in Christ who intend to visit the Holy Land. I prayerfully thought about what was said to me by one of the Ministers of God who was in my travelling party in November 2022 before embarking on this project. She was among the forty pilgrims that travelled to the Holy Land with me at the time. I believe strongly in my heart that the Lord was very gracious to us throughout the pilgrimage period, and we were tremendously blessed. It was from there that God inspired the Minister to call my attention to write this book. Considering how it happened, I can say it was like planting a seed in a good and well prepared soil when she called my attention to what has become the book in your hand—Praise the Lord!

On my part after we returned from the Holy Land, the thoughts about writing this Prayer Book became heavy on my heart and intense each time people called to share testimonies. The more I tried to block the thoughts about writing this book from my mind, the heavier it came back until I said to the Lord around January 2023, that I would write it and that was when I felt at peace in my heart. My desire and prayer after the decision to write this book is that, let everyone across the globe that would read and use this book for their prayers wherever and whenever, experience and have unique encounter with the God of Israel, be blessed tremendously as we were—even more in the name of Jesus Christ of Nazareth. Let me sign off with this Bible passage, (Numbers 33:1-2):

These are the journeys of the children of Israel, who went out of the land of Egypt by their armies under the hand of Moses and Aaron. 2 Now Moses wrote down the starting points of their journeys at the command of the LORD. ...

Let us journey to The Holy (Promised) Land, mentally and physically and tap into the riches and the blessedness of the promises of God for all His children.

INTRODUCTION

It has pleased God to use me to provide you with some Holy Spirit-led material, revelatory explanations and inspired prayer points at every Section of this book. My heartfelt prayer for you is that whether you use this book at home, during your Retreat or as one of your supporting materials at the Holy Land, you will receive miracles in the name of Jesus Christ. It is important you get all your travel documents required for your spiritual pilgrimage ready and up to date, but do not neglect the spiritual aspect which this book can play in your life. Please take a copy with you.

My prayer for you is that, your return from the Holy Land or your Retreat would be an enriching and testimony-filled experience to be enjoyed throughout your entire life, that you would have a deeper spiritual depth and wisdom more than before, far greater spiritual and physical results for God's Kingdom, and many other things that would benefit you, your generation and many generations to come, in the name of Jesus Christ.

Further advice for you, ensure you read the relevant Section(s) I have provided to acquaint yourself before your arrival at the holy site(s). Alternatively, you can read the necessary Sections to broaden your knowledge in general. As you would find out, I intentionally provided detailed explanations wherever I deemed necessary and important so to do. I testify to God's glory that for a decade now, each of my spiritual pilgrimage to the Holy Land results in various miracles, yours will not be an exception.

Also, I have had the privilege of travelling to The Holy Land for my personal spiritual pilgrimage several times, or led groups of Christian pilgrims independently, yet each visit is never the same. Therefore, I urge you to use this book (Prayer Rain) to pray fervently while in The Holy Land for your miracles. It can equally be used during your Retreat, or at home. As you would find out from this book—the Prayer points are designedly produced for each holy site for your ease and convenience.

Furthermore, this Prayer book is a useful intercessory material and helpful for your daily prayer life. It is intentional that each section of the book is arranged to be on a stand-alone format. What to do? Simply, choose the relevant section, open your heart prayerfully, release your faith, and connect to Yahweh—the God of Israel, put your trust in Him and He will not fail to answer you. Remember (Psalm 50:15; Jeremiah 33:3), the Bible reads;

Call upon Me in the day of trouble; I will deliver you, and you shall glorify Me.

Psalm 50:15

Call to Me, and I will answer you, and show you great and mighty things, which you do not know. Jeremiah 33:3

To conclude, not everyone that travels to The Holy Land desires to pray like you would like to do. Be aware of this important piece of advice because I experienced it with some people. Truly, some people go there on a holiday, for educational or research purposes, or sight-seeing—respect them and their choice. What to do? Try and avoid distraction and confrontation as much as possible. Don't give the devil a chance. Again, respect everyone for their opinion or the choice they have made. My guess is that, you are travelling to Israel on a spiritual pilgrimage or a Retreat, and you are determined to have an encounter with the God of Israel— focus on Him like the lame man at the Beautiful Gate (Acts 3:2-8) and receive your miracles.

And a certain man lame from his mother's womb was carried, whom they laid daily at the gate of the temple which is called Beautiful, to ask alms from those who entered the temple; 3 who, seeing Peter and John about to go into the temple, asked for alms. 4 <u>And fixing his eyes on him, with John, Peter said, "Look at us." 5 So he gave them his attention, [focus] expecting to receive something from them</u>. 6 Then Peter said, "Silver and gold I do not have, but what I do have I give you: In the name of Jesus Christ of Nazareth, rise up and walk." ... leaping up, he stood and walked. Acts 3:2-8.

Reverend Dr Isaac Ajibolorunrin

SECTION ONE

THE TRIUMPHAL ENTRY AND PALM SUNDAY PATH

The omniscient God is at work again as we shall soon read about how Jesus embarked on a journey to Jerusalem where the Messiah would be cut off as historically prophesied in (Daniel 9:26a) which reads; "And after the sixty-two weeks, Messiah shall be cut off, but not for Himself." It is understandable that in life people want to be successful and try to access their destiny to the fullest, but they have to start from somewhere—Jesus did, and that place is called Bethphage. The location was about two miles to His final destination which was around Jerusalem.

Traditionally, Bethphage was where Jesus' triumphal entry to Jerusalem began (Matthew 21:1) with a kind of festive atmosphere with people throwing their clothes of various colours, shapes and sizes on the donkey and the colt. Others cut branches from trees and spread them on the road, it is not surprising that in some places till today fresh branches from palm trees are being used to commemorate that historical moment of the triumphal entry of Christ. Note-worthily, those who went in front and those who followed were shouting Hosanna (Matthew 21:9), which means 'save us now.' Perhaps they meant to say to Jesus, 'save us now from our Roman oppressors.' Does that mean the crowd was completely ignorant of Jesus' mission? Not really so, because at some stage they said, "Blessed be the One who comes in the name of the Lord," which confirms their awareness of Jesus'

Messiaship. However, as time went on, 'hosanna' became an exclamation for praise.

As imaginable as possible of a festive arena, the vicinity transformed and became enlivened, noisy and joyous-like as recorded in (Matthew 21:1-15). The Bible passage is provided below. Has this tradition stopped, forgotten or how is it celebrated? At present, this event (the triumphal entry to Jerusalem) has not stopped, but is celebrated on Palm Sunday which usually is a week before Easter. It is worth remembering as stated in the narrative that Jesus calls Himself— King as He rode to the city, and that is reminiscent of how king David rode into Jerusalem in the past as a military-king after conquest.

However, no matter how it is considered, the triumphal ride by Jesus at this time was that of the Messiah emphasising His spiritual kingdom, and He was humble as symbolised by riding on a donkey and not on a military horse. If He rode on a horse, it could have passed as a political revolution like that of king David. Unfortunately, some of the multitudes that hailed Him (Jesus), or shouted 'Hosanna' would soon be in disagreement, desert Jesus and bow to political pressure and get Him killed, but we know He rose again. Hallelujah!

The Scripture: Matthew 21:1-3, 8-9

Now when they drew near Jerusalem, and came to Bethphage, at the Mount of Olives, then Jesus sent two disciples, 2 saying to them, "Go into the village opposite you, and immediately you will find a donkey tied, and a colt with her. Loose them and bring them to Me. 3 And if anyone says anything to you, you shall say, 'The Lord has need of them,' and immediately he will send them." … 8 And a very great multitude spread their clothes on the road; others cut down branches from the trees and spread them on the road. 9 Then the multitudes who went before and those who followed cried out, saying:

"Hosanna to the Son of David! 'Blessed is He who comes in the name of the LORD!' Hosanna in the highest!" Matthew 21:1-3, 8-9

Reflective Exercise

Jesus said to two of His disciples in the narrative:

"Go into the village opposite you, and immediately you will find a donkey tied, and a colt with her. Loose them and bring them to Me. 3 And if anyone says anything to you, you shall say, 'The Lord has need of them,' and immediately he will send them," Matthew 21:2-3

Some people thought it was pre-arranged. Not only that, the statement which says, "if anyone says anything to you, you shall say, 'The Lord has need of them,' and immediately he will send them." A School of thought argued this was a Password. How horrendous people can be?

In today's world, there are those who can downplay people's calling, ministry, ability, success, business achievements, or endowments, and they won't stop until their target (the person) becomes frustrated, discouraged, weak or useless. What to do? Be prayerful, be wiser, stay strong, remain focused at all times, learn from Jesus' example and make your main goal or assignment your Number One priority. If an attempt was made to diminish Jesus' supernatural power or knowledge, definitely we have a challenge on our hands and we need to pray. Some even thought Jesus sent the disciples to go and commandeer the animals. All this tend to show how wrong assumptions can jeopardise or truncate good intentions and the move of the supernatural.

If something like that happened to you before, it will never happen again in the name of Jesus Christ. Theologically, Jesus could be exercising His Right of

Requisition (Greek: *angareia*), which royalty or rabbis uses. Let us remember that Jesus is the King of kings and as a royal, He qualifies to exercise His Right of Requisition—and He did. Another key fact that should be borne in mind is that, the donkey was required for "a divine service" and there is no doubt about that, because Jesus used it exactly as prophesied and expected of Him, (Zechariah 9:9).

> Rejoice greatly, O daughter of Zion! Shout, O daughter of Jerusalem! Behold, your King is coming to you; He is just and having salvation, Lowly and riding on a donkey, A colt, the foal of a donkey. Zechariah 9:9

In context, they were being encouraged in the Old Testament by this promise of the Coming Messiah during that time, and this grace is what has happened in the New Testament which is called the Triumphal Entry.

Conversely, supposed that 'donkey tied' was the resources, line of credit, or opportunity you need for your job, business, ministry, etc., and is not forthcoming, would you keep quiet? The correct answer is emphatically No. Or, as a business person your products for sale are not being sold as expected, or trading well, would you look away? Again, the response to this question should be unquestionably No. Another question, as a Minister of God, if your Ministry is not growing or prospering, won't you be concerned? Definitely, you know you should turn to God in prayers and that is the right thing to do. Please aim to pray all the below prayer points aggressively.

Key Verse: You will find a <u>donkey tied,</u> and a colt with her. <u>Loose them and bring them to Me</u>. 3 <u>And if anyone says anything to you</u>, you shall say, 'The Lord has need of them,' and immediately he will send them. Matthew 21:2b-3

Enter Your Prayer Chamber

Powers that tie people to their ugly past, break into pieces over my life in the name of Jesus Christ

— Break into pieces now in the name of Jesus (repeat 3x)

Powers that tie people to their ugly past, as if there is no God in their life, I declare you null and void in my life in the name of Jesus Christ

— Break into pieces now and burn totally to ashes in the name of Jesus Christ (repeat 3x)

Powers that tie people to their ugly past, I am not your candidate — Catch fire now and burn to ashes

— Concerning my business, catch fire now and burn to ashes
— Concerning my ministry, catch fire now and burn to ashes
— Concerning my marriage, catch fire now and burn to ashes in the name of Jesus Christ

Powers that waste people's time and resources, I am not your candidate, catch fire and burn to ashes

— Concerning my career, catch fire and burn to ashes
— Concerning my prayer life, catch fire and burn to ashes in the name of Jesus Christ

Powers that want to confine me to unfruitful circumstances, you are a liar, be roasted by fire and burn beyond repair

— Concerning my health, burn beyond repair (repeat 3x)
— Concerning my finances, burn beyond repair in the name of Jesus Christ (repeat 3x)

From today, I loose all the resources required for my destiny-assignment from wherever they have been tied in the name of Jesu Christ

- All the resources locate me now in the name of Jesus Christ (repeat 7x)

I loose all the resources required for my destiny-assignment from whatever that is keeping them away from me in the name of Jesus Christ

- I loose them now in the name of Jesus (repeat 7x)

I terminate all opposition against the resources required to fulfil my destiny-assignment in my ministry in the name of Jesus Christ

- All opposition terminate now! (repeat 7x) in the name of Jesus Christ

I terminate all opposition against the resources required to fulfil my destiny-assignment in my vocation in the name of Jesus Christ

- All opposition terminate now! (repeat 7x) in the name of Jesus Christ

I terminate all confrontations against the opportunities that can help me to fulfil my destiny-assignment regarding my career

- All confrontations terminate now! (repeat 7x) in the name of Jesus Christ

I terminate all confrontations against the resources that can assist me to fulfil my destiny-assignment in my business

- Terminate in the name of Jesus Christ (repeat 7x)

I demolish all physical difficulties against the connections that can help to fulfil my destiny-assignment in the name of Jesus Christ

— Be demolished now! (repeat 7x) in the name of Jesus Christ

I crush all bureaucratic challenges against the connections that can help me to fulfil my destiny-assignment

— Be crushed now! in the name of Jesus (repeat 7x)

I command every spiritual difficulties against the contacts meant to enable me to fulfil my destiny-assignment to be destroyed

— Be destroyed in the name of Jesus Christ (repeat 7x)

Divinely-prepared answers that will shut down the arrangements of all my opponents be revealed to me from this moment

— Be revealed to me in the name of Jesus Christ (repeat 3x)

From today, I receive Divinely-inspired answers that will silence all my opponents permanently in the name of Jesus Christ

I receive it Lord, in the name of Jesus Christ

Forces of inactivity working against any aspect of my testimonies, your time is over! In the name of Jesus Christ of Nazareth,

— Loose your grip and power being used against me (repeat 7x) in the name of Jesus Christ

Forces of stagnancy working against any aspect of my success, your time is over! In the name of Jesus Christ of Nazareth, destroy yourselves

— Destroy yourselves in the name of Jesus Christ (repeat 7x)

Forces of darkness holding me down like the 'donkey tied' on the same spot, by the power and authority in the name of Jesus Christ, I break loose

— I break loose from now (repeat 7x) in the name of Jesus Christ

Powers that downplay people's ability—lose your potency over my life in the name of Jesus Christ

— Lose your hold now in the name of Jesus Christ (repeat 7x)

Powers that downgrade people's potentials—lose your influence over my life now!

— Lose it now, in the name of Jesus Christ (repeat 7x)

Powers that underrate people's endowment, be paralysed in my life in the name of Jesus Christ

Be paralysed now! (repeat 7x) in the name of Jesus Christ

Powers that minimise people's glorious gifts—lose your control over my life in the name of Jesus Christ

— Lose control now! (repeat 7x)

Powers that waste people's glorious talents—lose your power and authority over my life in the name of Jesus Christ

— Lose your power and authority over my life now! in the name of Jesus Christ

Powers that wickedly dilute people's glory— lose your strength over my life in the name of Jesus Christ

- Lose your strength now! (repeat 7x)

Agents of darkness, hired to circulate wrong rumours against my destiny-assignment, receive your shame right now in the name of Jesus Christ

- Receive your shame right now!(repeat 7x) in the name of Jesus Christ

Agents of darkness assigned to slander my family receive sudden disgrace right now in the name of Jesus Christ

- Receive sudden disgrace in the name of Jesus Christ (repeat 7x)

Agents of darkness assigned to slander my business receive unexpected disgrace right now in the name of Jesus Christ

- Receive unexpected disgrace in the name of Jesus Christ (repeat 7x)

Evil personalities assigned to quench the glory of my household, receive massive disappointment now in the name of Jesus Christ

- Receive big disappointment and failure (repeat 7x) in the name of Jesus Christ

Evil personalities assigned to defame my ministry, fail suddenly in your evil mission in the name of Jesus Christ

- Fail suddenly! (repeat 7x) in the name of Jesus Christ

Agents of darkness assigned to smear my career receive compounded shame right now in the name of Jesus Christ

— Receive compounded shame (repeat 7x) in the name of Jesus Christ

Personalities from the kingdom of darkness who circulate fake and wicked news to tarnish destiny-assignment, receive disappointment regarding my life in the name of Jesus Christ

— Receive disappointment regarding my life and my family (repeat 7x) in the name of Jesus Christ

My "tools" for divine service — locate me by fire!

(Name the "tools" for example: academic degrees, financial resources, building property, divine gifts, contacts at the appropriate level in political government, business and social services, etc.,)

— Locate me now! (repeat 7x) in the name of Jesus Christ

My "tools" for Calling into Ministry — locate me by fire!

(Name the "tools" for example: Genuine worshippers, God-fearing individuals, divine gifts, certificates from training courses, financial resources, building facilities, contacts at the appropriate level in political government, business and social services, etc.,)

— Locate me now! (repeat 7x) in the name of Jesus Christ

My "tools" for secular vocation — locate me by fire!

(Name the "tools" for example: trusted individuals, loyal staff, helpful financial institutions, landed property, government agencies, etc,.)

— Locate me now! (repeat 7x) in the name of Jesus Christ

Reference Scripture

> 6 So the disciples went and did as Jesus commanded them. 7 They brought the donkey and the colt, laid their clothes on them, and set Him on them. Matthew 21:6-7

Jesus did not sit on the two animals but the colt (Mark 11:2), because the mother was there to provide reassurance to avoid panic, or eliminate fear that could make the colt stray among the noisy crowd. You will never walk alone in the name of Jesus Christ.

Enter Your Prayer Chamber

O Lord my Father, from today don't let me walk alone all the days of my life in the name of Jesus Christ

- — Don't let me walk alone my Father in the name of Jesus Christ (repeat 7x)
- — Don't let me lack good companion in the name of Jesus Christ (repeat 7x)
- — Grant me healthy material support in the name of Jesus Christ
- — Don't let me lack genuine human help my Father, in the name of Jesus Christ
- — Don't let me lack authentic spiritual help my Father, in the name of Jesus Christ
- — Don't let me lack good and worthy assistance in the name of Jesus Christ
- — Grant me God-fearing comforters in the name of Jesus Christ

As the donkey accompanied her colt— Almighty God I pray, let your presence accompany me wherever I go, all the days of your life

- — Divinely accompany me any where I go my Father (repeat 3x) in the name of Jesus Christ

Almighty Father, permit your presence to be with me wherever I may be, all the days of my life in the name of Jesus Christ

Almighty Father, please don't allow your presence to depart from me all the days of my life in the name of Jesus Christ

Reference Scripture: Matthew 21:12-13

12 Then Jesus went into the temple of God and <u>drove out all those who bought and sold in the temple</u>, and <u>overturned the tables of the money changers</u> and the seats of those who sold doves. 13 And He said to them, "It is written, 'My house shall be called a house of prayer,' but you have made it a 'den of thieves. Matthew 21:12-13

Reflective Exercise

The Temple's outer court was turned to a commercial market — imagine market stalls, hawkers' tables owned by the money-changers, chairs and benches scattered all over! As if not enough, think about stables for goats, sheep and cages for birds for sale to their 'customers' scattered around the entire vicinity. Also, consider the stench from the urine and excrements of the sacrificial animals that most likely filled the air, and birds excrement in their cages in the trading areas which was part of the Temple.

Definitely, all this would have made the Temple's surroundings turned to eyesore. Apart from the entire environment being noisy caused by hagglers, traders and buyers, the worshipper-buyers, were compelled by circumstances beyond their control to buy from the Temple traders at exorbitant prices. Could the worshippers truly and genuinely have enjoyed the spiritual experience they came for? Beyond any doubt, there is need for action.

Furthermore, if the worshippers intended to convert other currencies to Shekel (the native and legal tender at the time in Israel, even till today), to enable them to pay for their Temple tax, the money-changers would charge excessive commission or interest which was unfair. Not only unfair, but it constituted the desecration of the Temple. Hear this, disappointingly, commercial activities were given priority over sacred activities. Where were the Temple priests? Have they connived with the traders in their illicit trade? The implication simply is that, resulting from the above factors, the Temple had become unsuitable for its original purpose which was to be a place for worshipping God, but now has been turned to "den of robbers instead of a House of Prayer."

Let the truth be told, the responsible individuals had become corrupt, selfish and were after their personal material gains. Candidly, they were exploiting the pilgrims. How would you feel if someone valued their monetary benefits above you and your family's well-being, spiritual life, ministry and business interests? Again, how would you feel if you were treated dishonourably in regards to what you cherish? What about someone converting your property (life, marriage, profession etc.,), to another purpose for their selfish interests? Nobody likes that. The Temple was overdue for cleansing. Conversely, in our personal lives I think it would be a nice idea to ask God to visit us constantly with His cleansing power because our bodies represent the temple of God. Before too late let us get ready to pray.

Enter Your Prayer Chamber

My Father and my God, please visit me with your cleansing power regularly and cleanse me thoroughly in the name of Jesus Christ

— The Holy One of Israel, please cleanse me all over again! (repeat 7x) in the name of Jesus Christ

— Cleanse me inside-out my Father and my God (repeat 7x) in the name of Jesus Christ

My Father and my God, please visit my family constantly with your cleansing power and cleanse us in the name of Jesus Christ

My Father and my God, please visit my ministry regularly with your cleansing power and cleanse us in the name of Jesus Christ

— Cleanse us thoroughly (repeat 7x) in the name of Jesu Christ

My Father and my God, please visit my business on a constant basis with your cleansing power and cleanse us in the name of Jesus Christ

Every agenda of Destiny-manipulators concerning my life— scatter and burn to ashes in the name of Jesus

— Scatter and burn to ashes in the name of Jesus (repeat 7x)

Every agenda of Destiny-manipulators concerning my success— scatter and burn to ashes in the name of Jesus

— Scatter and burn to ashes in the name of Jesus (repeat 7x)

Powers that reverse destiny and glory for evil, stop operating in my life from today in the name of Jesus Christ

— Stop operating in my marriage from today in the name of Jesus Christ
— Stop operating in my children's life from today in the name of Jesus Christ

— Stop operating in my spouse's life from today in the name of Jesus Christ
— Stop operating in the life of my loved ones from today in the name of Jesus Christ

Powers that reverse favour for evil, stop operating in my life from today in the name of Jesus Christ

— Stop operating in my marriage from today in the name of Jesus Christ
— Stop operating in my children's life from today in the name of Jesus Christ
— Stop operating in my spouse's life from today in the name of Jesus Christ

Powers that reverse victory for evil, stop operating in my life from today in the name of Jesus Christ

— Stop operating in my marriage from today in the name of Jesus Christ
— Stop operating in my children's life from today in the name of Jesus Christ
— Stop operating in my spouse's life from today in the name of Jesus Christ

Powers that reverse wealth for poverty, stop operating in my life from today in the name of Jesus Christ

— Stop operating in my marriage from today in the name of Jesus Christ
— Stop operating in my children's life from today in the name of Jesus Christ
— Stop operating in my spouse's life from today in the name of Jesus Christ

Powers that reverse breakthrough for evil, stop operating in my life from today in the name of Jesus Christ

— Stop operating in my marriage from today in the name of Jesus Christ

- Stop operating in my children's life from today in the name of Jesus Christ
- Stop operating in my spouse's life from today in the name of Jesus Christ

In the name of Jesus Christ of Nazareth, every shame organised against me and my family fall back on the perpetrators

- Fall back on them (perpetrators) in the name of Jesus

In the name of Jesus Christ of Nazareth, every disgrace organised against me and my family fall back on the perpetrators

- Fall back on them (evil organisers) in the name of Jesus (repeat 7x)

In the name of Jesus Christ of Nazareth, let the backwardness organised against me and my family fall back on the organisers without fail

- Fall back on them (all the wicked organisers) in the name of Jesus

In the name of Jesus Christ of Nazareth, let the failure organised against me and my family fall back on all the evildoers suddenly

- Fall on them (all the evildoers) in the name of Jesus (repeat 7x)

In the name of Jesus Christ, the Son of the Living God, I command all the false allegations organised against me and my business to fall on all the satanic organisers

- Fall on them (all my persecutors) in the name of Jesus (repeat 7x)

I command all the embarrassment organised against me and my ministry to fall on all the satanic organisers in the name of Jesus Christ

— Suddenly fall on them! (repeat 7x)

All satanic organisers working against my life and ministry, the Hand of God is against you from today in the name of Jesus Christ

I command all the wickedness organised against me and all my loved ones to fall on the satanic organisers in the name of Jesus Christ

— Back fire in the name of Jesus Christ! (repeat 7x)

All conspirators (satanic companions) seeking my downfall, fall into every pit you have dug for me in the name of Jesus Christ of Nazareth

— Fall into it (repeat 7x) the pit they have dug for me)

I command all the backwardness the Devil intended for me and my family to fall on the people behind it in the name of Jesus Christ

— Fall back on them (repeat 7x)

I command the barrenness the Devil intended for me and my household to fall back on the people behind it

— Fall back on them (repeat 7x) in the name of Jesus Christ

I declare in the name of Jesus Christ that the barrenness the Devil intended for me and my business fall back on the people behind it

— Fall back on them! (repeat 7x) in the name of Jesus Christ

I command any power that wants to reverse God's intended purpose for my life to discontinue their evil plan suddenly, in the name of Jesus Christ

— Discontinue now in the name of Jesus Christ (7x)

Powers! bent on dishonouring me and my family for monetary gain, be rendered powerless forever from this minute in the name of Jesus Christ

— Be rendered powerless in the name of Jesus Christ (repeat 7x)
— Let their power base be broken into pieces in the name of Jesus Christ
— Be broken into pieces (repeat 7x)

Powers! bent on dishonouring me and my ministry for monetary gain, scatter by fire! in the name of Jesus Christ

— Scatter by fire in the name of Jesus Christ (repeat 7x)

I render powerless every agent of darkness bent on sabotaging me and my business for monetary gain in the name of Jesus Christ

I render powerless all agents of darkness bent on using my situation to enrich themselves in any form or shape, in the name of Jesus Christ

From today, let all evil agents who are bent on subverting me and my family for their popularity become powerless in the name of Jesus Christ

— Be powerless in the name of Jesus Christ

From this moment, let all evil agents who are bent on subverting me and my family for their self-importance become powerless in the name of Jesus Christ

From today, let all evil agents who are bent on subverting me and my career for their advantage become powerless in the name of Jesus Christ

Every agenda of Satanic-converters concerning my life— scatter! and catch fire in the name of Jesus Christ

— Scatter and catch fire! (repeat 7x) in the name of Jesu Christ

Every agenda of Satanic-converters concerning my destiny—scatter and catch fire in the name of Jesus Christ

— Scatter and catch fire! (repeat 7x)

The Lord of hosts! Please deliver me from the hands of Satanic-converters who are bent on frustrating the original purpose of my life

— Deliver me O Lord in the name of Jesus Christ (repeat 7x)

Almighty Father, rescue me and my household from the hands of Satanic-polluters taking advantage of my life in the name of Jesus Christ

— Great Deliverer! Rescue me in the name of Jesus Christ (repeat 7x)

Great and Mighty God, rescue me and my household from the hands of Demonic destiny-exchangers who take advantage of people against their will

— My Great Deliverer, deliver me in the name of Jesus Christ (repeat 7x)
— My Great Deliverer rescue me in the name of Jesus Christ (repeat 7x)

Go ahead and give thanks to God for answering your prayers, magnify His holy name and worship Him, believe that He has answered your prayers according to what He said in (Mark 11:23-25):

> For assuredly, I say to you, whoever says to this mountain, 'Be removed and be cast into the sea,' and does not doubt in his heart, but believes that those things he says will be done, he will have whatever he says. 24 Therefore I say to you, whatever things you ask when you pray, believe that you receive them, and you will have them. Mark 11:23-25.

SECTION TWO

MOUNT CARMEL

ELIJAH — THE HUMAN AGENT
AND GOD'S SERVANT

By default or supernatural-design, you would find out that in life things are bound to happen beyond human control. Irrespective, as a child of God we are encouraged to continue to seek His face until things get better. Although life can be challenging in several ways, but God can channel all the difficulties to fulfil His divine purposes. Again as we continue to pray and trust in Him, let us remember that He always uses human agents as He pleases. For instance, Elijah was one of them. God can use anybody to accomplish various tasks and goals and we don't have to understand Him all the time.

As an individual, family or ministry, you can commit yourself to Him and be ready to share a serious and deep relationship with Him like Elijah did. When Elijah committed himself to Yahweh, he was able to perform great miracle— you too can expect answered prayers, amazing results and extra-ordinary miracles from God.

To recall, we found in (1 Kings 17:1) that this prophet called Elijah was introduced simply as God's prophet from Tishbite. Is that all? But nothing was said about his background and family, or how he was called to the prophetic ministry. However, it was clear from his performances that he was God's chosen vessel, raised to bring the adulterous and prideful Israel back to God. Notably, he called for drought (1 Kings 17:1b), and fire which symbolised the wrath, or divine judgment of God and it happened, (1 Kings 18:24, then 36-39). As recorded, later his prayers resulted to rain which typifies blessing (1 Kings 18:45).

Enter Your Prayer Chamber

Lord God of Elijah! from today turn me to a "global-vessel" and use me all the days of my life

Lord God of Elijah! from today, turn me to a "global-shaker" and use me for your glory all the days of my life

Father, let me be a unique "ground-breaker" (pioneer) in the destiny you have formed for me in the name of Jesus Christ

- — Father, let me be a groundbreaker (repeat 7x) in the name of Jesus Christ
- — Father, let me be a trailblazer (repeat 7x) in the name of Jesus Christ

Lord God of Elijah! from today, let me and my household be a significant instrument for you all the days of our lives

Lord God of Elijah! from today, let me and my household belong to "a class of distinction" for your glory and praise

God of Elijah! from today, let me be a terror to those terrorising my life and my household in the name of Jesus Christ

O Lord, make me a terror to all my terrorisers in the name of Jesus Christ (repeat 7x)

Reference Scripture: 1 Kings 18:24, 36-39

24 Then you call on the name of your gods, and I will call on the name of the LORD; and the God who answers by fire, He is God." So all the people answered and said, "It is well spoken."... 36 And it came to pass, at the time of the offering of the

evening sacrifice, that Elijah the prophet came near and said, "LORD God of Abraham, Isaac, and Israel, let it be known this day that You are God in Israel and I am Your servant, and that I have done all these things at Your word. 37 Hear me, O LORD, hear me, that this people may know that You are the LORD God, and that You have turned their hearts back to You again." 38 Then the fire of the LORD fell and consumed the burnt sacrifice, and the wood and the stones and the dust, and it licked up the water that was in the trench. 39 Now when all the people saw it, they fell on their faces; and they said, "The LORD, He is God! The LORD, He is God!" ... 45 Now it happened in the meantime that the sky became black with clouds and wind, and there was a heavy rain. So Ahab rode away and went to Jezreel. (1 Kings 18:24, 36-39, 45).

Enter Your Prayer Chamber

God of Elijah! Please settle my case by fire!

— Settle my case by fire! (repeat 7x) in the name of Jesus Christ

God of Elijah! intervene decisively in my case

— Intervene by fire (repeat 7x) in the name of Jesus Christ

God of Elijah! let me experience your sudden intervention in the presence of all my enemies regarding ... (marriage, career, ministry, finance, health, promotion, in parenting my children, etc.,)

God of Elijah! please grant me miracles that will mock all my enemies from today in the name of Jesus Christ

God of Elijah! grant me extraordinary miracles where it matters most in my life, in the name of Jesus Christ

God of Elijah! grant me "first-of-its-kind" miracles from today, in the name of Jesus Christ

God of Elijah! grant me "first-of-its-kind" healing from today, in the name of Jesus Christ

God of Elijah! grant me "first-of-its-kind" deliverance from today, in the name of Jesus Christ

God of Elijah! grant me "first-of-its-kind" victory from today, in the name of Jesus Christ

God of Elijah! grant me "first-of-its-kind" prosperity from today, in the name of Jesus Christ

God of Elijah! grant me "first-of-its-kind"favour from today, in the name of Jesus Christ

God of Elijah! grant me "first-of-its-kind" breakthroughs from today, in the name of Jesus Christ

God of Elijah! grant me "first-of-its-kind" success from today, in the name of Jesus Christ

Unquestionable miracles from the Lord! be my portion from this moment in the name of Jesus Christ of Nazareth

Elijah's Encounter with the Priests of Baal on Mount Carmel

At Muhraka

At the highest point or peak of the stretches of the mountains which is called Muhraka, was the venue of the contest. The Mediterranean sea till today is fairly visible from this location. It was from its direction that Elijah's servant saw a cloud which was rising from the sea like a man's hand (1 Kings 18:43-44) and turned to a heavy rain later.

> And said to his servant, "Go up now, look toward the sea." So he went up and looked, and said, "There is nothing." And seven times he said, "Go again." 44 Then it came to pass the seventh time, that he said, "There is a cloud, as small as a man's hand, rising out of the sea!"... 1 Kings 18:43-44

However, it should be noted that the weather can be hazy occasionally which means that visibility can be poor and people won't be able to spot what they would have wished. In such condition, what serves better as a landmark to help identify where the Mediterranean sea is situated, are some tall chimneys which emit smoke to the sky once the generating plants are working. Back to Muhraka, the floor of the elevated terrace is clearly marked with directional names already inscribed on the floor. The diagram which is like a directional compass is provided to help pilgrims or tourists have an idea about where to locate places of interest apart from where the Mediterranean sea can be located.

Let us recall that Elijah represented God during the time of the contest, but the four hundred and fifty prophets of Ahab represented Baal. It should also be remembered that the agreement was, the "deity" of whoever won the contest would be known as the Supreme Being— for us, He is Yahweh and for the other party, Baal. When Elijah prayed on that day God answered and fire fell from heaven, my prayer for you is God will answer you today in the name of Jesus Christ. Elijah cherished the occasion because God gave him victory and he was able to mock the prophets of Baal on that day, so you shall begin to mock your enemies openly from now onwards in the name of Jesus Christ. As an endorsement of Elijah's ministry and an acknowledgement that God was on Elijah's side, the testimony is that, suddenly God revealed Himself in form of a fire which fell from heaven on that day. I pray for you that unexpectedly, God will manifest Himself in your situation in the name of Jesus Christ. Just believe and have faith.

Reflective Exercise

Supposing your life, business, ministry or project was faced by some challenges, intimidation, or a stiff and detrimental competition, opposition, a serious threat, or a dilemma that can terminate everything, what would you do? The last option is for you to fold your arms and keep watching— only an insane person would do that. Notice from the below narrative that God can answer us in dramatic and spectacular ways. How soon would you like to pray your way through for your breakthrough? I suggest you start from now.

Reference Scripture

> 22 Then Elijah said to the people, "I alone am left a prophet of the LORD; but Baal's prophets are four hundred and fifty men. 23 Therefore let them give us two bulls; and let them choose one bull for themselves, cut it in pieces, and lay it on the wood, but put no fire under it; and I will prepare the other bull, and lay it on the wood, but put no fire under it. 24 Then you call on the name of your gods, and I will call on the name of the LORD; and the God who answers by fire, He is God." So all the people answered and said, "It is well spoken." 1 Kings 18:22-24

Enter Your Prayer Chamber

Elijah asked for fire (a symbol of judgement) while on the mountaintop, right now ask personally for your own "fire" that will settle your matter— Pray like this:

O Lord God of Elijah! Settle my case by fire! (repeat 7x)

- — Settle me personally
- — Settle me matrimonially
- — Settle me in regards to raising my children, preserve them for me, don't let them be a bad influence, don't let them be wayward, let them be good example throughout their lives, don't let them cause me pain or sorrow in the name of Jesus Christ

O Lord God of Elijah!

— Settle me medically throughout my lifetime and don't allow my health to fail me
— Settle me regarding Court cases and in all legal issues
— Settle me in regards to all financial matters
— Settle me mentally and emotionally
— Settle me physically and psychologically
— Settle me spiritually
— Settle me vocationally
— Settle me in my career
— Settle me academically (please pray for all our students)
— Settle me in all my endeavours and never let me be put to shame in the name of Jesus Christ.

Elijah's trademark or popular sign was 'fire'— Pray like this: My Father and my God, give me my own "logo" before I leave this place of prayer (Mount Carmel) today

Almighty Father please grant me a 'special trademark' which will glorify your name in every aspect of my life

Almighty God, you were on Elijah's side and gave him testimony by the sign of fire, because of Your mercy, give me testimony by fire regarding my entire life from today in the name of Jesus!

— Testimony by fire! be my portion (repeat 7x) in the name of Jesus Christ

O God of Elijah! grant me a special symbol of distinction that will never allow my life to remain the same again —

— Special mark that will not allow my family to be the same again
— Special symbol that will prevent my job from being the same again

- — Special mark that will not let my business remain the same again
- — Special sign that will not allow my ministry to be the same again
- — Special mark that will not permit my finances to be the same again
- — Special 'fire' that will not allow my health to deteriorate in the name of Jesus Christ.

The fire that came down on Mount Carmel was also a sign of endorsement of Elijah's ministry, my Father and my God, send down your fire of endorsement upon my life.

Please sing this Chorus at least (repeat 3x), if you know it:

Send down fire
Holy Ghost fire
Send down fire again
Holy Ghost fire

Pray like this:

Lord God of Elijah! send down your fire of endorsement of victory upon every aspect of my life— Suddenly!

- — Anywhere I may go
- — Anywhere I may be
- — And for all times to glorify your name in the name of Jesus Christ of Nazareth

Lord God of Elijah! send down your fire of endorsement of deliverance upon every aspect of my life— Suddenly!

- — Anywhere I may go
- — Anywhere I may be
- — Any day as may be required for me and my spouse
- — And for all occasions to glorify your name in my life in the name of Jesus Christ

Lord God of Elijah! send down your fire of endorsement of breakthrough upon every aspect of my life— Suddenly!

— Anywhere I may go
— Anywhere I may be with my children
— And for each day of my life in the name of Jesus Christ

Lord God of Elijah! send down your fire of blessings upon every aspect of my life— Suddenly!

— Anywhere I may be with all my loved ones
— Any time to glorify your name
— And all over my life in the name of Jesus Christ

Lord God of Elijah! send down your fire of endorsement of good health upon every aspect of my life— Suddenly!

— Anywhere I may go
— Anywhere I may be
— Any time to glorify your name
— And all over my life and my family in the name of Jesus Christ of Nazareth

Lord God of Elijah! send down your fire of prosperity upon every aspect of my life, and let me prosper suddenly!

— Anywhere I may be
— Any day as required
— And all over my life and my ministry in the name of Jesus Christ

Lord God of Elijah! send down your fire of success upon every aspect of my life, and let me be successful!

— Anywhere I may be
— Any day as required
— And all over my life and my business in the name of Jesus Christ

My Father and my God, you intervened for Elijah and he was not disgraced, please intervene for me throughout my entire life in the name of Jesus Christ

— Intervene for me spiritually, physically and in any form or shape necessary (repeat 3x) in the name of Jesus Christ

Psalm 27:10 says, "When my father and my mother forsake me, then the LORD will take care of me."

— Do not neglect me O God, (repeat 3x) in the name of Jesus Christ

Elijah's God took care of him by using fire to acknowledge that He (God) was on Elijah's side. He is ready to do His miracles in your life today. Hallelujah!

Please sing this song at least (repeat 3x) if you know it, or recite it:

God that answereth by fire O
Let Him be my God
God that answereth by fire O
Let Him be my God

Jehovah answereth by fire O
Let Him be my God
Jehovah answereth by fire O
Let Him be my God

Yahweh answereth by fire O
Let Him be my God
Yahweh answereth by fire O
Let Him be my God

Pray like this:

Lord God of Elijah! please use your supernatural intervention (fire) to turn things around for my good, for the sake of your Name

O Lord God of Elijah! use your fire to settle my case— come rain, come sunshine

O Lord God of Elijah! use your fire to settle my case— in whatever situation I might be going through

Fire of favourable acknowledgement from God— be my portion (repeat 3x) in the name of Jesus Christ

Fire of God! consume any power contending with me, my marriage and my children in the name of Jesus Christ

Fire of God! let all powers contending with me, my next level and promotion be consumed by fire in the name of Jesus Christ

Powers contending with me because of my glorious destiny!

— Be consumed by fire (repeat 3x) in the name of Jesus Christ

Powers contending with me because of my contacts and connections!

— Be consumed by fire(repeat 3x) in the name of Jesus Christ

Powers contending with me as a result of my job, career or business!

— Be consumed by fire (repeat 3x) in the name of Jesus Christ

All powers contending with me because of my Calling and Ministry!

— Be consumed by fire (repeat 3x) in the name of Jesus Christ

Powers contending with me in order to rubbish my Calling and Ministry, you are a liar!

— Be consumed by fire (repeat 7x) in the name of Jesus Christ

Powers contending with me in order to waste my time, Calling and Ministry!

— Be roasted by fire (repeat 7x) in the name of Jesus Christ

Every prophet of Baal assigned to pull me down from my place of blessing— receive open and public disgrace from this minute in the name of Jesus Christ

— Receive open and public disgrace (repeat 7x) in the name of Jesus Christ

Every prophet of Baal assigned to pull me down from my spot of honour— receive open and public disgrace from this moment in the name of Jesus Christ

— Receive open and public disgrace (repeat 7x) in the name of Jesus Christ

Every prophet of Baal assigned to pull me down from my place of favour— receive open and public disgrace straightaway in the name of Jesus Christ

— Receive open and public disgrace (repeat 7x) in the name of Jesus Christ

Every prophet of Baal assigned to pull me down from my point of success— receive open and public disgrace now in the name of Jesus Christ

— Receive open and public disgrace (repeat 7x) in the name of Jesus Christ

Every prophet of Baal assigned to pull me down from my place of breakthrough— receive open and public disgrace immediately in the name of Jesus Christ

— Receive open and public disgrace (repeat 7x) in the name of Jesus Christ

Every prophet of Baal assigned to pull me down from my height of glory, your time is over!

— Receive open open and public disgrace now (repeat 7x) in the name of Jesus Christ

All prophets of Baal sent on evil assignment against my life, terminate yourself from this day in the name of Jesus Christ

— Terminate yourself (repeat 7x) in the name of Jesus Christ

All prophets of Baal at my place of work and their forces working against my opportunities therein, terminate yourself from this day in the name of Jesus Christ

— Terminate yourself (repeat 7x) in the name of Jesus Christ

Every prophet of Baal operating at my place of employment and their forces working against my advancement therein, terminate yourself from today in the name of Jesus Christ

— Terminate yourself (repeat 7x) in the name of Jesus Christ

Prophets of Baal at my place of work supported by other wicked external forces looking for my downfall, your time is over— be roasted by fire!

— Be roasted by fire (repeat 7x) in the name of Jesus Christ

Prophets of Baal on evil assignment against my marriage, terminate yourself from this minute in the name of Jesus Christ

— Cease to operate (repeat 7x) in the name of Jesus Christ

Prophets of Baal on evil assignment against my children, terminate yourself from this moment in the name of Jesus Christ

— Terminate yourself (repeat 7x) in the name of Jesus Christ

Prophets of Baal that colluded with my ancestral root working against my life and destiny, cease to operate from this minute

— Cease to operate forever (repeat 7x) in the name of Jesus Christ

Prophets of Baal in my blood line who imposed barriers against my progress in life, terminate yourself and let the barriers be broken into pieces from this day in the name of Jesus Christ

— Every barrier be broken (repeat 7x) in the name of Jesus Christ

Prophets of Baal in my blood line collaborating with external forces of darkness so as to hinder my progress in life, your time is up!

— Terminate yourself right now (repeat 7x) in the name of Jesus Christ,

Prophets of Baal collaborating with internal and external forces of darkness, assigned to hinder my family and marriage— your reign is over!

— Turn powerless immediately (repeat 7x) in the name of Jesus Christ

Prophets of Baal collaborating with internal and external forces of darkness, assigned to hinder my business and investments, your reign is over!

— Terminate yourself now (repeat 7x) in the name of Jesus Christ

Prophets of Baal collaborating with internal and external forces of darkness appointed to hinder my assignment on earth, your rule is over!

— Cease to operate in my life from today (repeat 7x) in the name of Jesus Christ

Prophets of Baal in my blood line supported by other wicked external forces looking for my downfall, your time is over!

— Be roasted by fire! (repeat 7x) in the name of Jesus Christ

Prophets of Baal in my blood line sponsored by other wicked external forces looking for my death, your reign is over!

— Back to sender! (repeat 7x) in the name of Jesus Christ of Nazareth

Prophets of Baal in my blood line sponsored by other wicked external forces wanting me to die prematurely, your rule is over!

— Die instead of me (repeat 7x), Psalm 118:17. I ...... (mention your name) shall not die, but live to declare the works of God in the name of Jesus Christ

Agents of Baal in alliance with other wicked external forces looking for the death of my spouse and children you are a liar!

— Die instead of us (repeat 7x) in the name of Jesus Christ

Representatives of Baal in collaboration with other wicked external forces looking for my death and the death of my loved ones your time is over!

— Die instead of us (repeat 7x) in the name of Jesus Christ

That Power of God that brought fire from heaven on Mount Carmel!
   Bring judgment on all my enemies from this minute in the name of Jesus Christ

— Bring judgment on them O Lord (repeat 7x) in the name of Jesus Christ

The Power of Yahweh that brought fire from heaven on Mount Carmel!

— Fight for me … (mention your name) in regards to … (fruit of the womb, financial difficulties, health problems, etc., mention the challenge), in the name of Jesus Christ

The Power of Jehovah that brought fire from heaven on Mount Carmel!
   Disgrace speedily all those waging war against my life

— Disgrace them my Father (repeat 7x) in the name of Jesus Christ

That Power of God that brought fire from heaven on Mount Carmel!
   Settle my case in regards to … (Please mention the challenge, for example, financial debts, career progression, education, contract, marriage, ministry, business contracts, health etc,.).

— The LORD, strong and mighty in battle— settle my case (repeat 7x) in the name of Jesus Christ

The Power of Jehovah that brought fire from heaven on Mount Carmel!

Takeover every battle in my life and give me victory

— Takeover, the LORD of hosts (repeat 7x) in the name of Jesus Christ

That Power of God of Elijah that brought fire from heaven on Mount Carmel!

Takeover every battle in my lineage and give me victory

— Takeover, the LORD of hosts (repeat 7x) in the name of Jesus Christ

The Power of Yahweh that brought fire from heaven on Mount Carmel!

Make public show of all my enemies from now onwards in the name of Jesus Christ of Nazareth

— Give them public disgrace Jehovah (repeat 7x) in the name of Jesus Christ

The Power of Jehovah that brought fire from heaven on Mount Carmel!

Intervene for me and transform my life completely in the name of Jesus Christ

— Transform my business
— Transform my ministry
— Transform my marriage etc., in the name of Jesus Christ
— Intervene O LORD my Father (repeat 7x) in the name of Jesus Christ

That Power of God that brought fire from heaven on Mount Carmel!

Advertise God's glory in my life immediately in the name of Jesus Christ

— Advertise yourself O Lord as the glory and the lifter of my head (repeat 3x) in the name of Jesus Christ

God of Elijah who sent fire from heaven on Mount Carmel! Advertise your glory in my family from today in the name of Jesus Christ

— Advertise yourself as the strong and mighty God in my family (repeat 3x) in the name of Jesus Christ

That Power of Yahweh that brought fire from heaven on Mount Carmel!
Don't allow my glory to be wasted in the name of Jesus Christ

— Don't allow my glory to be wasted (repeat 7x) in the name of Jesus Christ

That Power of Jehovah that brought fire from heaven on Mount Carmel!
Don't allow my glory to be inherited by another person in the name of Jesus Christ

— Don't allow my glory to be inherited (repeat 7x) in the name of Jesus Christ

That Power of Jehovah that brought fire from heaven on Mount Carmel!
Don't allow my glory to be snatched away by another person in the name of Jesus Christ

— Don't allow my glory to be snatched away (repeat 7x) in the name of Jesus Christ

The Power of God that brought fire from heaven on Mount Carmel!

Don't allow my life to remain the same again from today in the name of Jesus Christ

- — Don't allow my life to remain the same again (repeat 7x) in the name of Jesus Christ

The Power of God of Elijah that brought fire from heaven on Mount Carmel!

- — Advertise God's power in my life, as all power belongs God (Psalm 62:11)
- — Advertise yourself in my life, Lord God Almighty (repeat 7x) in the name of Jesus Christ

The Power of Almighty God that brought fire from heaven on Mount Carmel!

Let my life be meaningful from today, as originally destined for me in the name of Jesus Christ of Nazareth

The Power of Almighty God that brought fire from heaven on Mount Carmel!

Don't allow my life to be wasted in any form or shape, in the name of Jesus Christ

- — As God lives, my life will not be wasted in any form or shape (repeat 7x) in the name of Jesus Christ
- — As God lives, my opportunities will not be wasted in any form or shape (repeat 7x) in the name of Jesus Christ

Jeremiah 29:11, "For I know the thoughts that I think toward you, says the LORD, thoughts of peace and not of evil, to give you a future and a hope."

Mention your name and pray like this: Father, let my entire life replicate the good plans you have ordained for me from today in the name of Jesus Christ

The Power of God of Elijah that brought fire from heaven on Mount Carmel! Attend to all my situation and give me testimony in the name of Jesus Christ

— Ground-breaking testimony from Jehovah, come and be my portion from today (repeat 7x) in the name of Jesus Christ
— Ground-breaking testimony from Yahweh, continue to be my portion in the name of Jesus Christ of Nazareth (repeat 7x)

Divine rainfall like on the day at Mount Carmel! Fall and quench every drought in my life—

— Fall and quench drought for my marriage and children
— Fall and quench drought for me medically and financially
— Fall and quench drought for me vocationally
— Fall and quench drought for all my endeavours in the name of Jesus Christ.

* Thank God for answering your prayers, sing songs of praise and adoration to Him, and look forward to His miracles happening in your life soonest. Remember to share the testimony of God's goodness at all times, God bless you.

SECTION THREE

THE PLACE OF ASCENSION

THE DIVINE SPACE CENTRE —
LUKE 24 50-52

Jesus' ascension to heaven is incomparable to any religious leader ever known, there is nothing like it. Undoubtedly, for we Christian believers, no technological, mechanical or scientific explanations can be sufficiently rendered to make us think Jesus was not lifted to heaven supernaturally. As supernatural it was for Him to be lifted to heaven, so it was when He was supernaturally raised from the dead (resurrection) in three days as He predicted— "Destroy this temple, and in three days I will raise it up." (John 2:19). Furthermore, no engineering coalition or alliance, nor joint sponsorship like some countries have done by launching their satellites into Space (International Space Station), can compare to the Ascension of Jesus Christ. The Ascension was supernatural hence I refer to it as the divine space centre.

Briefly, let us consider for example, what it takes for a Space travel in the present day to take place, although Jesus' ascension was more than a Space travel. Normally for a modern day Space travel, there would be a great excitement whenever a rocket is to be launched into Space. The launch without doubt, would attract the attention of the public, businesses and possibly governments at any particular time. Jesus' ascension unfortunately did not make the headlines of the newspapers during the time when it happened.

How much did it cost in monetary terms in regards to Jesus' lift-off not to Space but heaven? It is beyond human estimation and comprehension what took place on that glorious day. However, it takes so much preparation, work or labour hours and expertise for the unprecedented scientific device called Spacecraft or Spaceship to orbit Earth. It is expensive in monetary terms, it costs billions in United States currency, (Dollar). And there is a risk of everything blowing up in a split second during, or after take-off, particularly when the rocket fails to deploy. But the ascension story was a successful one. Shockingly, as the disciples stood there in amazement because of how Jesus was lifted to heaven, they were told Jesus would come back again (Acts 1:10-11), Hallelujah!

10 And while they looked steadfastly toward heaven as He went up, behold, two men stood by them in white apparel, 11 who also said, "Men of Galilee, why do you stand gazing up into heaven? This same Jesus, who was taken up from you into heaven, will so come in like manner as you saw Him go into heaven. Acts 1:10-11

Space Travel and the Ascension Not the Same

In general, although sad to say, but the collaborated efforts for the Space travel, despite their engineering, scientific and technological exercises, all could be aborted without a remedy due to any eventuality— follow my story patiently. The best they could do is to muster strength again and go back after they have overcome their disappointment and loss. But, the Ascension experience was not like that. Furthermore, a lot of background work would have been done for Space Travel to take place prior to the time of lift-off or launching their rocket. Amongst others, the Control room staff with all kinds of computers, screen monitors with different sizes and shapes would have been configured for various purposes with each team member assigned to one task or the other. Any of the team members who fails to perform their roles as expected can lead to a disaster. Therefore, there has to be a proper order of things, for instance, all trained members of staff for the project and their related specialists with assigned roles have to work seamlessly as a team throughout— intra and inter-departmentally.

Additionally, the crew or the astronauts would have been quarantined for some time to avoid contamination, placed on special diets prior to the launch date, and they have to wear special suits fitted with their oxygen tubes and communication gadgets for contacts between the Space station and the Control Centre on earth, and vice versa. Everything has to be scientifically precise before the day of the launch. It is when all these arrangements have been concluded that they would take off. Does this compare in any way to the Ascension? Emphatically NO. Again, no one can with certainty guarantee success till they return to earth as scheduled. Can you imagine the extent people had to go for this human project which is susceptible, or not fail-proof?

Certainly, this differs entirely from how Jesus was lifted to heaven on that special day at a spot called the place of Ascension (Divine Launch Station) as recorded in (Luke 24: 50-51) which reads;

> 50 Then Jesus led them out along the road to Bethany, and lifting his hands to heaven, he blessed them, 51 and then began rising into the sky, and went on to heaven. Luke 24:50-51 TLB

At this divine Launch Station (The Place of Ascension), there were no computers, no Control room staff to help, no special Space suits to wear, Jesus needed not to be quarantined for weeks lest He becomes infected, and so on, but the mission took place successfully.

Enter Your Prayer Chamber

Unusual grace that leads to Divine lifting, be my portion from today in the name of Jesus Christ (repeat with the below outlined prayer points)

— Unusual grace for divine lifting be my portion in my life in the name of Jesus Christ
— Uncommon grace for divine lifting be my portion in my family in the name of Jesus Christ
— In my career, let unique grace divinely lift me up in the name of Jesus Christ
— In my business, let unusual grace divinely raise my business in the name of Jesus Christ
— In my ministry, let extraordinary grace divinely enlarge the ministry in the name of Jesus Christ
— In my calling, let unusual grace divinely do unusual miracles in the name of Jesus Christ
— In my finances, let uncommon grace divinely provide for me in the name of Jesus Christ

By the reason of divine lifting, let uncommon grace locate me from today in the name of Jesus Christ;

— Divine lifting for my promotion, locate me from today in the name of Jesus Christ:
— Divine lifting - locate me for good health,
— Divine lifting - locate me for my marriage
— Divine lifting - locate me for my investment
— Divine lifting - locate me for my education
— Divine lifting - locate me for my Ministry in the name of Jesus Christ

Extraordinary divine lifting from Jehovah! Take me to my glorious heights from this moment in the name of Jesus Christ of Nazareth

— Take my wife to her glorious heights with ease
— Take my husband to his glorious heights without difficulty

- Take all my children to their glorious heights without trouble
- Take all my siblings to their glorious heights with comfort
- Take my entire household to our glorious heights without complications in the name of Jesus Christ
- Take my business to its glorious heights without delay in the name of Jesus Christ
- Take my ministry to its glorious heights without hesitation in the name of Jesus
- Take all my destiny-helpers to their glorious heights by divine speed in the name of Jesus.

* Thank God for answering your prayers, sing songs of praise and adoration to Him, and look forward to His miracles happening in your life soonest. Remember to share the testimony of God's goodness at all times, God bless you.

SECTION FOUR

THE CHURCH OF DOMINUS FLEVIT

WAR WAS INEVITABLE

This site provides a panoramic view of the then city of Old Jerusalem where Jesus stood at that time. It was from this distance that Jesus pronounced His lamentation over Jerusalem as recorded in (Luke 19:41-44). I pray that you will not walk blindly into your future. And you will not walk into a community laden with a curse. It would seem that the audience at the time Jesus was delivering this prediction never understood what He was telling them. The simplest way to put it is, war was inevitable. But one wonders if humans over generations are really ready to learn from the mistakes of others. Believe it or not, as time went on, the fulfilment of the prediction took place when a Roman military General called Titus surrounded the city. Not only that, he trapped all the inhabitants, both young and old and brutally massacred them. In addition, he completely destroyed the walls and all the buildings of the Old city.[1] Let us read the prediction as was foretold by Jesus Christ, (Luke 19:41-44);

41 Now as He drew near, He saw the city and wept over it, 42 saying, "If you had known, even you, especially in this your day, the things that make for

---

[1] William MacDonald, (Art Farstad ed.), *Believer's Bible Commentary — A Complete Bible Commentary in One Volume*, London: Thomas Nelson Publishers, 1995, p. 1443

your peace! But now they are hidden from your eyes. 43 For days will come upon you when your enemies will build an embankment around you, surround you and close you in on every side, 44 and level you, and your children within you, to the ground; and they will not leave in you one stone upon another, because you did not know the time of your visitation. Luke 19:41-44

The people of Jesus' day missed their golden opportunity when they refused to receive Jesus Christ as the Messiah. Is there any much difference between us today and the people in question? The truth is, not many want to accept Jesus as their Messiah even today, which means they are missing their golden opportunity too. Further, accepting Jesus Christ as their Messiah could have brought them at least their personal peace and secure their eternity in heaven. Unfortunately, they rejected Him. Truth be told, Jesus wailed over Jerusalem at that time because His offer of salvation was rejected. But the irony is that, how come the people who live at a place which has 'peace' (Salem, as part of its name), supposedly a city of peace rejecting peace? Or failed to receive the Prince of Peace, Isaiah 9:6b? Also, Ephesians 2:13-14a.

And His name will be called Wonderful, Counsellor, Mighty God, Everlasting Father, Prince of Peace... Isaiah 9:6b

13 But now in Christ Jesus you who once were far off have been brought near by the blood of Christ. 14 For He Himself is our peace, ... Ephesians 2:13-14a

What they failed to realise was that true peace demands that they as God's creature, maintain right relationship with their Creator. But they failed to understand, and all this brought tears to Jesus' eyes. It is my prayer that this time, no one would bring tears to Jesus' eyes.

Enter Your Prayer Chamber

As said earlier, the fulfilment of the prediction in (Luke 19:41-44) took place when General Titus surrounded the city. He trapped all the inhabitants, both young and old and brutally massacred them. Brothers and sisters, we need to pray that every city, neighbourhood, towns, etc., laden with curses will not have effect over us in the name of Jesus Christ. Amen.

— On the grounds of mercy and God's grace, I cancel any curse uttered against my village or town in the name of Jesus Christ of Nazareth
— Be cancelled in the name of Jesus Christ (repeat 7x)
— I decree that I will not be a partaker of such curses, my entire household and all my loved ones in the name of Jesus Christ
— I decree that my ministry, business and all my endeavours will not be a partaker of such curses in the name of Jesus Christ
— No matter how long ago, I terminate any curses placed on my community or neighbourhood by the Blood of Jesus Christ of Nazareth
— Terminate by the Blood of Jesus Christ (repeat 7x)
— All generational negative pronouncements hanging over my life, your time is over! In the name of Jesus Christ I command you to neutralise now by the Blood of Jesus Christ
— Neutralise now by the Blood of Jesus Christ! (repeat 7x)
— Every generational negative pronouncements hanging around my life, your time is over! I command you to neutralise now by the Blood of Jesus Christ
— Each generational negative pronouncements hindering my life, your time is over! In the name of Jesus Christ,

I command you to neutralise by the Blood of Jesus Christ

— Every generational negative pronouncements wasting my life, your time is over! I command you to neutralise now by the Blood of Jesus Christ and in the name of Jesus Christ

— All generational negative pronouncements frustrating my life, your time is over! In the name of Jesus Christ, neutralise now.

The Time of Your Visitation Has Come!

Let us consider this statement: ... Because you did not know the time of your visitation. Luke 19:44c

The time of visitation is that God's moment which things are bound to happen for your own good and several others that God has ordained for such. It is my desire that they would be positive ones in the name of Jesus Christ. Pray like this:

Almighty Father, from today please restore all my lost 'time of positive visitation' because of your mercy in the name of Jesus Christ of Nazareth.

— Restore me in the name of Jesus Christ (repeat 7x).

Mary's Time of Visitation

Let me digress a little, the Virgin Mary was one of the few people who never missed their time of visitation, (Luke 1:26-30). Looking into the entire story as recorded below, I can say that the entire episode was draped by grace, we all need grace.

26 Now in the sixth month the angel Gabriel was sent by God to a city of Galilee named Nazareth, 27 to a virgin betrothed to a man whose name was Joseph, of the house of David. The virgin's name

was Mary. 28 And having come in, the angel said to her, "Rejoice, highly favoured one, the Lord is with you; blessed are you among women!" 29 But when she saw him, she was troubled at his saying, and considered what manner of greeting this was. 30 Then the angel said to her, "Do not be afraid, Mary, for you have found favour with God. Luke 1:26-30

Please pray that during your time of visitation grace will complete the miracles for you.

— Father of all grace and mercy, please let your grace and mercy complete my allotted miracles this day for me in the name of Jesus Christ
— Father of all grace and mercy, let your grace and mercy complete your assigned plan and purposes in my life soonest, in the name of Jesus Christ
— O Lord! Let your grace work out your assigned plan and purposes seamlessly for my family and my business in the name of Jesus Christ
— Great and Mighty Father, let your grace work out your allotted plan and purposes seamlessly for my ministry and all endeavours in the name of Jesus Christ
— Almighty Father, because of your grace, please restore to me all my lost 'opportunity of favourable visitation' from today in the name of Jesus Christ of Nazareth

Jehovah, please bring back my "God's moment" and never allow my life to remain the same again ...

— Regarding my home
— Regarding my health
— Regarding my ministry
— Regarding my business
— Regarding my destiny
— Regarding my finances

— Regarding my promotion
— (add more prayers points as you deem fit), for I pray in the name of Jesus Christ of Nazareth!

Great and Mighty God, please bring back my "God's moment for good" and let my life be transformed completely in the name of Jesus Christ of Nazareth
Great and Mighty God, please bring back my "God's moment for good" and let my life be transformed physically and spiritually in the name of Jesus Christ of Nazareth

— And let my life be transformed financially and materially in the name of Jesus Christ of Nazareth
— And let my life be transformed medically to enjoy good health till the end of my life in the name of Jesus Christ of Nazareth
— Bring back all my "God's moment" because of your mercy (repeat 3x)
— Bring back all my "God's moment" because of your grace (repeat 3x), I pray in the name of Jesus Christ.

Serious Warning!

Don't Be Careless, you only have one life — pray like this:

O Lord my Father! Please don't let me walk blindly into my future in the name of Jesus Christ, people who walk blindly into their future never achieve in life

— Don't let my wife walk blindly into her future
— Don't let my husband walk blindly into his future
— Don't let my children walk blindly into their future
— Don't let all my siblings walk blindly into their future
— Don't allow any of my loved ones walk blindly into their future in the name of Jesus Christ of Nazareth

Merciful Father! help me to take care of all necessary warnings pertaining to my life and godliness in the name of Jesus Christ

- — Help my wife to take care of all necessary warnings pertaining to her life and godliness
- — Help my husband to take care of all necessary warnings pertaining to his life and godliness
- — Help all my children to take care of all necessary warnings pertaining to their life and godliness
- — Help all my siblings to take care of all necessary warnings pertaining to their lives and godliness
- — Help my household to take care of all necessary warnings pertaining to their lives and godliness

My Father in the name of Jesus, deliver me from all kinds of ignorance and carelessness, spiritually and mentally in regards to places we go to (repeat 7x)

Almighty Father in the name of Jesus, deliver me from all kinds of ignorance and foolishness, physically and financially in regards to our business projects (repeat 7x)

Lord, deliver all my family members from all kinds of ignorance and carelessness as we invest in one business or the other, in the name of Jesus Christ

Lord, deliver my ministry from all kinds of ignorance and stupidity henceforth in the name of Jesus Christ

Father, deliver all my ministry members from all kinds of ignorance and foolishness in decision-making in the name of Jesus Christ

My Deliverer, deliver my business from all kinds of ignorance and carelessness in choices that we make at all times in the name of Jesus Christ.

Jesus is Our Prince of Peace, Isaiah 9:6b

Lord my Father, please don't let me throw away the true peace that comes from you

— Don't allow my wife to throw away the true peace that comes from you
— Don't permit my husband to throw away the true peace that comes from you
— Don't let my children throw away the true peace that comes from you
— Don't let my siblings throw away the true peace that comes from you
— Don't allow my household members to throw away the true peace that comes from you in the name of Jesus Christ

Father God, don't allow my heart to be hardened towards the truth that will benefit me and my entire life in the name of Jesus Christ

Almighty God, don't allow the heart of my wife to be hardened towards the truth that will benefit her in the name of Jesus Christ

Gracious God, don't allow the heart of my husband to be hardened towards the truth that will benefit him in the name of Jesus

God my Father, don't allow the heart of my children to be hardened in relation to the truth that will benefit them in the name of Jesus Christ of Nazareth

God my Father, don't allow the heart of all my siblings to be hardened in regards to the truth that will benefit them in the name of Jesus Christ of Nazareth

Father God, don't allow the heart of all my loved ones to be hardened against the truth that will benefit them in the name of Jesus Christ of Nazareth.

* Thank God for answering your prayers, sing songs of praise and adoration to Him, and look forward to His miracles happening in your life soonest. Remember to share the testimony of God's goodness at all times, God bless you.

SECTION FIVE

THE GARDEN OF GETHSEMANE

Before the crucifixion of Jesus at Golgotha also known as the place of Skull, the Saviour of all mankind went to the Garden of Gethsemane to pray en-route the Mount of Olives. As one descends the slope from the Mount, and walks through the Palm Sunday Path which Jesus Himself trekked during that time, the Garden extends across the slope in your front. To be precise, the Church of All Nations is on the left hand side, while the Garden of Gethsemane stretches across the road on both sides. This particular environment is beautifully adorned with olive trees with a few of them dating back to Jesus' time which is amazing, there He agonised as recorded in (Luke 22:28-54).

The expanse of land on which the Garden occupies currently provides sections for personal or group prayer meetings, and spiritual pilgrims if so desired, can book spaces in advance for their quiet prayers, meditation and Communion services. For those who desire, they can enter the Church of All Nations built on some part of the rock of Agony purported to be where Jesus went to pray. As described by the evangelist, the distance between Jesus and the disciples was not far from each other, "it was a stone throw away" (Luke 22:41), that location is referred to as the rock of Agony.

After the overwhelming agony in spirit but still in the Garden, one of Jesus' disciples called Judas Iscariot (the Betrayer), came with a mob and betrayed Jesus through a kiss. It must be emphasised that the kiss was an agreed signal between Judas Iscariot and the mob, (Matthew 26:48). The mob was headed by the chief priests, captains of the Temple guards and the religious leaders. In a nutshell, that was how Jesus was arrested by the authorities. Let us read Luke 22:45-54:

45 When He rose up from prayer, and had come to His disciples, He found them sleeping from sorrow. 46 Then He said to them, "Why do you sleep? Rise and pray, lest you enter into temptation." 47 And while He was still speaking, behold, a multitude; and he who was called Judas, one of the twelve, went before them and drew near to Jesus to kiss Him. 48 But Jesus said to him, "Judas, are you betraying the Son of Man with a kiss?" 49 When those around Him saw what was going to happen, they said to Him, "Lord, shall we strike with the sword?" 50 And one of them struck the servant of the high priest and cut off his right ear. 51 But Jesus answered and said, "Permit even this." And He touched his ear and healed him. 52 Then Jesus said to the chief priests, captains of the temple, and the elders who had come to Him, "Have you come out, as against a robber, with swords and clubs? 53 When I was with you daily in the temple, you did not try to seize Me. But this is your hour, and the power of darkness." 54 Having arrested Him, they led Him and brought Him into the high priest's house. But Peter followed at a distance. Luke 22:45-54

Reflective Exercise

Take a moment to think about hostility, rejection, deception and betrayal by someone you love and trusted. Now, let's turn our attention to the following questions:

Have you been deceived by a loved one before? How would you have felt about the sudden deceptive attitude that Judas Iscariot showed to Jesus, if you were the person he did it to? When last did you experience hostility and how did you respond to it? Do you know what it means to be rejected? Have you experienced betrayal before? Would you ever wish to have a relationship with hypocrites? Can you cope with people who are pretenders? But Jesus went through all the above and many more because of the redemption of the souls of mankind.

Enter Your Prayer Chamber

Towards the end of His earthly journey, if Jesus had refused to die by way of crucifixion on the Cross, it would have been a case of "failure at the edge of success." At this point, I request that you pray against failure at the point of breakthrough, success and accomplishment as provided below:

Father, let every arrangement by the devil for me to fail at my point of breakthrough be roasted by fire! Be completely destroyed in the name of Jesus Christ!

I command all Satanic arrangements against my life to explode by fire!

All satanic wickedness against my life— burn to ashes beyond recognition in the name of Jesus Christ

— Explode by fire and burn to ashes in the name of Jesus Christ (repeat 7x)

Every Satanic arrangement for me to fail at the edge of success, I command you to explode by fire and burn to ashes in the name of Jesus Christ

Failure at the edge of breakthrough — I am not your candidate! In the name of Jesus Christ of Nazareth, catch fire and burn to ashes

— Catch fire and burn to ashes (repeat 7x) in the name of Jesus Christ

Failure at the edge of accomplishment— I am not your candidate! Be roasted by fire

56

- — I and my wife are not your candidate
- — I and my husband are not your candidate
- — I and my children are not your candidate
- — I and my household are not your candidate
- — My ministry is not your candidate
- — My business is not your candidate in the name of Jesus Christ!

Peter as a Target

31 And the Lord said, "Simon, Simon! Indeed, Satan has asked for you, that he may sift you as wheat. 32 But I have prayed for you, that your faith should not fail; and when you have returned to Me, strengthen your brethren." 33 But he said to Him, "Lord, I am ready to go with You, both to prison and to death." 34 Then He said, "I tell you, Peter, the rooster shall not crow this day before you will deny three times that you know Me." Luke 22:31-34

We read earlier that Satan targeted Peter "to sift him like wheat." Pray like this:

Any power targeting my life for evil be roasted by fire!

Any power targeting my family for evil— be destroyed totally in the name of Jesus Christ

- — Be destroyed in the name of Jesus Christ (repeat 7x)

Any power targeting my health for evil, be roasted by fire in the name of Jesus Christ

Powers that target ministry for evil, break into pieces concerning me and all my endeavours!

- — Break into pieces in the name of Jesus Christ (repeat 7x)

Any power targeting my business for evil, be roasted by fire!

Powers that target finances for evil, break into pieces concerning me and my household

— Break into pieces concerning me and my wife
— Break into pieces concerning me and my husband
— Break into pieces concerning me and my ministry
— Break into pieces concerning me and my business
— Break into pieces in the name of Jesus Christ (repeat 7x)

Judas Iscariot (the Betrayer)

Believe it or not, there comes a time that in people's life a "Judas Iscariot" will present himself or herself— it is a spirit. If it happened to Jesus Christ, it can happen to anybody, (Matthew 26:48).

48 Now His betrayer had given them a sign, saying, "Whomever I kiss, He is the One; seize Him." Matthew 26:48

All evil identification mark (a "kiss" on that occasion for Jesus), assigned against me in real life, (through my car, house, office, the colour of my dress, place of work, construction site, etc.,), cancel by the Blood of Jesus Christ!

— I cancel it now in the name of Jesus Christ (repeat 7x)

Evil marks placed on any aspect of my life directly or by proxy, reverse by the power in the Blood of Jesus!

— Reverse now (repeat 7x) by the power in the Blood of Jesus Christ

Every evil identification mark assigned against my family in the spirit-realm, terminate yourself by the Blood of Jesus Christ

— Terminate now (repeat 7x) in the name of Jesus Christ

All evil identification mark assigned to attack me in my dream— backfire in the name of Jesus Christ!

— Backfire now (repeat 7x) in the name of Jesus Christ

Every evil identification mark agreed against my ministry in the kingdom of darkness

— Blow up in their faces in the name of Jesus Christ
— Blow up in their faces (repeat 7x) in the name of Jesus Christ

Evil identification marks agreed against my business in the kingdom of darkness, your time is over! Turn powerless in the name of Jesus Christ

— Turn powerless (repeat 7x) in the name of Jesus Christ

Every 'Judas' (betrayer or traitor) around my life (male or female), but behaving like a saint, you are a liar! Be exposed and be defeated from today in the name of Jesus Christ

— Be exposed and be defeated (repeat 7x) from today, in the name of Jesus Christ

Every betrayer (young or old) around my destiny, but behaving like an innocent person, be disgraced and be defeated from today in the name of Jesus Christ

Every traitor (Judas) around my glory, but behaving like a friend, be disgraced and be defeated from today in the name of Jesus Christ of Nazareth

Every household wickedness working against my rising, but behaving like a true friend, be disgraced and be defeated from today in the name of Jesus Christ

Every satanic informant around my household, but behaving like an innocent person, be exposed and be disgraced from today in the name of Jesus Christ

— Be exposed and be disgraced (repeat 3x) in the name of Jesus Christ

Arrow of wickedness— return to your sender in the name of Jesus Christ

Arrow of untimely death— return to your sender in the name of Jesus Christ

Arrow of backwardness— return to your sender in the name of Jesus Christ

Arrow of cancerous diseases — return to your sender in the name of Jesus Christ

Arrow of persecution— return to your sender in the name of Jesus Christ

Arrow of hatred— return to your sender in the name of Jesus Christ

Arrow of rejection— return to your sender in the name of Jesus Christ

Arrow of hostility— return to your sender in the name of Jesus Christ

Arrow of betrayal— return to your sender in the name of Jesus Christ

Arrow of evil load — return to your sender in the name of Jesus Christ

Arrow of sorrow— return to your sender in the name of Jesus Christ

Arrow of wickedness— return to your sender in the name of Jesus Christ

Arrow of barrenness— return to your sender in the name of Jesus Christ

Arrow of failure at the brink of breakthrough— return to your sender in the name of Jesus Christ!

Almighty Father, please give me extra strength to face and conquer every challenge around my life in the name of Jesus Christ

Almighty Father, please give me extra strength to face and defeat every challenger around my life in the name of Jesus Christ

The "cup" was inescapable for Jesus

The 'cup' metaphorically was a terrible agony with horror which would befall Jesus at some point in His life, but He was committed to it and God gave Him strength. Pray like this:

God my Father, from today please strengthen and give me victory over all challenges ahead of my life in the name of Jesus Christ

— Strengthen and grant me victory (repeat 7x) in the name of Jesus Christ

Almighty God, whatever the agony around me, help me to be victorious in the name of Jesus Christ

Almighty Father, whatever the challenges around my life, help me to be victorious in the name of Jesus Christ

The Lord of hosts, whatever the challenges around my family, help us to be victorious in the name of Jesus Christ

Almighty Father, whatever the challenges around my ministry, help me to be victorious in the name of Jesus Christ

Thou God of the the armies of Israel! (1 Samuel 17:45), whatever the challenges around my business, help me to be victorious in the name of Jesus Christ

Almighty Father, you are the Man of war, the LORD is Your name, (Exodus 15:3), whatever the challenges around my career, help me to be victorious in the name of Jesus Christ

— Any time, any day and all the days of my life, my Father let me be victorious in the name of Jesus Christ

The Strength of Israel, (1 Samuel 15:29), please help my faith to be strong in the name of Jesus Christ

— Help my faith to be strong O Lord (repeat 7x) in the name of Jesus Christ

Abba Father, help me to re-affirm my commitment to you like Jesus did in the Garden of Gethsemane (Matthew 26:42)

— Help me my Father in the name of Jesus Christ

Jehovah, the Stone of Israel (Genesis 49:24), please keep me going Lord — no matter what! I pray in the name of Jesus Christ

— Keep me going Lord (repeat 7x) in the name of Jesus Christ

LORD I pray, in my place of assignment don't let me give up in the name of Jesus Christ (Matthew 26:44)

— I refuse to quit (repeat 7x) in the name of Jesus Christ

Thou Holy One of Israel! (Isaiah 30:15), please don't let me be faint-hearted in my place of assignment in the name of Jesus Christ

— Father, don't let me be confused
— Don't let me be gullible
— Don't let me be vulnerable
— Don't let me be discouraged
— Don't let me be distracted in the name of Jesus Christ of Nazareth

Evil Alliance

Judas Iscariot came with *"a mob ..."* (Matthew 26:48a). The "mob" comprised of the chief priests, captains of the Temple guards and the religious leaders. This was an alliance purposely formed to arrest Jesus Christ in the night to face their Kangaroo Court. Similarly, we cannot rule out satanic alliance or coalition to promote evil deeds against God's children in today's world. As God's children we need to pray without ceasing (1 Thessalonians 5:17), so we can remain victorious. Please pray like this:

Every satanic alliance (mob), bent on pulling me down in my profession, scatter in the name of Jesus Christ

— Scatter in the name of Jesus Christ (repeat 7x)

All satanic alliance that doesn't want me to excel in life, you are a liar! I command such evil confederation to be aborted in the name of Jesus Christ

— Be aborted (repeat 7x) in the name of Jesus Christ

All satanic coalition and evil connections aimed at me be aborted in the name of Jesus Christ (repeat 7x)

Evil Signal

Now His betrayer had given them a sign, saying, "Whomever I kiss, He is the One; seize Him." Matthew 26:48

It is unfortunate but true, that some people make wicked arrangements in secret and cause havoc, or death to their fellows by agreeing on a sign to be used to attack their victim(s). Sadly, the unfortunate individuals might not even know they bear such evil marks, or the direction which the danger would be coming from. I command such mark or sign to be erased completely from our midst in the name of Jesus Christ of Nazareth. Pray like this:

Every satanic signs and marks meant to truncate my life— be erased by the Blood of Jesus Christ!

— Be erased permanently (repeat 7x) in the name of Jesus Christ

Satanic signs and marks meant to truncate my star— be erased by the Blood of Jesus Christ

— Be erased now (repeat 7x) in the named Jesus Christ

All satanic signs and marks meant to truncate my glory! Your time is over

— Be erased by the Blood of Jesus Christ (repeat 7x)

Every satanic signs and marks meant to truncate my assignment in life

— Be erased by the Blood of Jesus Christ (repeat 7x)

Every agreed sign or mark organised against me by evil agents— directly or indirectly, backfire openly!

— Backfire openly (repeat 7x) in the name of Jesus Christ

Arrest in the Night

The religious leaders did not arrest Jesus in the Temple where they knew people would riot because of Jesus' innocence, hence they came in the night. Can we call that an unguarded hour? Of course, not for Jesus, because He was aware of their evil plan ahead of time. As it turned out, the religious leaders knew their target and agreed on a time for action. Who have made you their target, and what have been their scheduled time for attack or atrocities to commence? They (evil agents) will fail woefully in the name of Jesus Christ. Pray like this:

In the name of Jesus, all agents of Satan I am not your target!

— My wife is not your target
— My children are not your target

- My business is not your target
- My ministry is not your target
- Every aspect of my life is not your target in the name of Jesus Christ

Every satanic timing aimed at causing havoc against my life— crash completely in the name of Jesus Christ

- Crash completely (repeat 7x) in the name of Jesus Christ

All satanic arrangements aimed at causing havoc against my profession— you are a liar!

- Crash totally in the name of Jesus Christ
- Crash completely (repeat 7x) in the name of Jesus Christ

Every satanic timing aimed at causing havoc against my household—

- Crash completely in the name of Jesus Christ

All satanic timing aimed at causing havoc against my Ministry—

What are waiting for? Crash completely in the name of Jesus Christ

- Crash completely now (repeat 7x) in the name of Jesus Christ

Every satanic network organised to cause havoc against my business—

- Crash completely in the name of Jesus Christ
- Crash permanently in the name of Jesus Christ (repeat 3x). Thank you King of kings, because I know you have heard me and my victory is settled in the name of Jesus Christ of Nazareth.

* Thank God for answering your prayers, sing songs of praise and adoration to Him, and look forward to His miracles happening in your life soonest. Remember to share the testimony of God's goodness at all times, God bless you.

SECTION SIX

MOUNT SINAI

Mount Sinai peninsula occupies about 60,000 square kilometres land mass and shares its borders with Egypt, Syria, Jordan and Israel. It is accessible through any of the mentioned nations with each claiming to be a part of the sacredness of the mountain. However, Egypt is the most popular of them and the venerated site can be accessed through Saint Catherine monastery. In the Bible, Mount Sinai has been called interchangeably by other names in the past. For example, Horeb (the mountain of God, Exodus 18:5), this was where Moses saw a bush burning but it was not consumed (Exodus 3:1-2, 12; 4:27; 24:13; 33:6; 1 Kings 19:8). It has also been called the Mountain of the LORD (Numbers 10:33).

3 Now Moses was tending the flock of Jethro his father-in-law, the priest of Midian. And he led the flock to the back of the desert, and came to Horeb, the mountain of God. 2 And the Angel of the LORD appeared to him in a flame of fire from the midst of a bush. So he looked, and behold, the bush was burning with fire, but the bush was not consumed, ... 12 So He said, "I will certainly be with you. And this shall be a sign to you that I have sent you: When you have brought the people out of Egypt, you shall serve God on this mountain." Exodus 3:1-2, 12

33 So they departed from the mountain of the LORD on a journey of three days; and the ark of the covenant of the LORD went before them for the

three days' journey, to search out a resting place for them. Numbers 10:33

Where is Mount Sinai now?

As arguably stated by Menachem Posner, at present "the location did not maintain its holiness and cannot be pinpointed with relative certainty."[2] Nevertheless, it must be understood that the biblical references in the Old Testament and the relevance of the divine events during that time shaped the world of the population which existed at that period. Furthermore, the few selected agents of Yahweh, the God of Israel who received revelations and were permitted to play key roles, for instance, Moses and Elijah impacted the world around them. All this have huge implications for Christian believers in today's world. Therefore, when people try to visit, or go on a spiritual pilgrimage to the holy site as we have seen in the past, and till now we should not be surprised. For me, God's specific and extraordinary supernatural circumstances like clouds, thunderings, lightning, smoke and fire as in (Exodus 20:18-19) that were shown through His agents in regards to Mount Sinai remain timeless.

18 Now all the people witnessed the thunderings, the lightning flashes, the sound of the trumpet, and the mountain smoking; and when the people saw it, they trembled and stood afar off. 19 Then they said to Moses, "You speak with us, and we will hear; but let not God speak with us, lest we die." Exodus 20:18-19

Note-worthily, the intention of the seekers or those who embark on a spiritual pilgrimage to the holy site is not

2 Article by Menachem Posner in Chabad.org (chabad.org/library/article_cdo/aid/5115389/jewish/9-facts-You-Should-Know-About-Mount-Sinai.htm). Cited on 16/07/2023

about God who is resident-based, or locally based there, but God, the Omnipresent One who at some point in history manifested Himself in visible signs and memorable forms with spiritual implications for both then, and now for His practitioners— Mount Sinai is one of such places where people of the past were struck with fear, trembling and awe. The holy site (Mount Sinai) undoubtedly is venerated by the Jewish and Christian traditions, and the Muslims too.

It is important to mention that Mount Sinai, Mount Zion and Mount Sion are not the same, and should not be confused from each other. The difference can be made clearer through biblical stories that would be provided as we go along. From the biblical account, we realise that Moses and the Israelites had an encounter with God in a practical way on Mount Sinai (Exodus 19:17-19), but at other times Moses met God alone (Exodus 34:1-2). Further, Moses was alone when he first received from God the two tablets containing the Ten Commandments (Exodus 20:18-19), but it was later reviewed in (Deuteronomy 5:1-22, see Appendix 1) with the entire assembly in attendance.

17 And Moses brought the people out of the camp to meet with God, and they stood at the foot of the mountain. 18 Now Mount Sinai was completely in smoke, because the LORD descended upon it in fire. Its smoke ascended like the smoke of a furnace, and the whole mountain quaked greatly. 19 And when the blast of the trumpet sounded long and became louder and louder, Moses spoke, and God answered him by voice. Exodus 19:17-19

34 And the LORD said to Moses, "Cut two tablets of stone like the first ones, and I will write on these tablets the words that were on the first tablets which you broke. 2 So be ready in the morning, and

come up in the morning to Mount Sinai, and present yourself to Me there on the top of the mountain. Exodus 34:1-2

18 Now all the people witnessed the thunderings, the lightning flashes, the sound of the trumpet, and the mountain smoking; and when the people saw it, they trembled and stood afar off. 19 Then they said to Moses, "You speak with us, and we will hear; but let not God speak with us, lest we die." Exodus 20:18-19

Enter Your Prayer Chamber

Pharaoh's daughter had her plans for Moses but God had to intervene. Pray like this:

My Father, please direct my steps back to my glorious destiny from today in the name of Jesus Christ

— Direct my steps O God (repeat 7x) in the name of Jesus Christ

Moses unintentionally killed an individual which made him to be a wanted felon, he lost his adopted status and privileges at the palace and was wanted for the murder he committed. Pray like this:

— Change and elevate my status from today LORD, in the name of Jesus Christ
— In your mercy LORD, change and enrich my profile from today in the name of Jesus Christ

Father, please change my profession from a shameful one to honourable one in the name of Jesus Christ

Like Moses, God Almighty remove me from all unprofitable career and business for a better one

— Remove me Lord (repeat 7x) in the name of Jesus Christ

Moses was being raised as a potential king (Pharaoh), but due to circumstances he became a shepherd and worked for his father in-law. But remember, it was God who took Moses from Mount Sinai to lead the Israelites, (Exodus 3:10). Pray like this:

Lord, take me from where I am now, to where I am supposed to be in the name of Jesus Christ

— Take me before too late LORD, (repeat7x) in the name of Jesus Christ

Father, don't allow the potential you have invested in me be wasted in the name of Jesus Christ

God of Abraham, don't allow the talents you have blessed me with be wasted in the name of Jesus Christ

God of Isaac, don't allow the anointing you have endowed on my life be wasted in the name of Jesus Christ

God of Jacob, don't allow the wisdom you have blessed me with be wasted in the name of Jesus Christ

Is the law of the land against you? When Moses returned to Egypt the murder case had expended. Pray like this. Thou Great Judge! Discharge and acquit me of all spiritual and legal cases in the name of Jesus Christ

— Vindicate me of all cases Jehovah (repeat 7x) in the name of Jesus Christ
— Set me free from all cases Jehovah (repeat 7x) in the name of Jesus Christ

Moses had his mountain-top experience at Mount Sinai and his life changed, pray like this:

My mountain-top encounter!

— Locate me and transform my life now! (Repeat 7x)

— Locate me and transform my life today! (repeat 7x) in the name of Jesus Christ.

* Thank God for answering your prayers, sing songs of praise and adoration to Him, and look forward to His miracles happening in your life soonest. Remember to share the testimony of God's goodness at all times, God bless you.

SECTION SEVEN

BIBLICAL NARRATIVES OF MOUNT ZION

There are many ways to look at the name of this mountain called Mount Zion. This mountain has been variously described through several traditions and historical stories. However, I have intentionally limited my discourse within the Old and New Testaments of the Bible. Therefore, I believe this material comes to my readers in the most direct way. Firstly, Mount Zion was used to refer to the City of David which was located outside the Old City walls. For an example, Kind David's tomb and the Cenacle can be found there. Secondly, this mountain is said to be part of the hill on which the Temple Mount is situated and thirdly, the iconic Golden Dome is within the same vicinity. Not the least, one of the fundamental facts is that the holy site is venerated by practitioners of three faiths namely, Judaism, Christianity and Islam. Further, this holy site is held as the third most sacred in Islam apart from Mecca and Medina.

Notwithstanding, it is believed that this was where Abraham went to sacrifice Isaac as God instructed. In the Bible, the place is called Mount Moriah (Genesis 22: 2-4). All this tends to show how over some period of time the so-called Mount Zion has been variously named.

2 Then He (God) said, "Take now your son, your only son Isaac, whom you love, and go to the land of Moriah, and offer him there as a burnt offering on one of the mountains of which I shall tell you." 3 So Abraham rose early in the morning and

saddled his donkey, and took two of his young men with him, and Isaac his son; and he split the wood for the burnt offering, and arose and went to the place of which God had told him. 4 Then on the third day Abraham lifted his eyes and saw the place afar off. Genesis 22:2-4

Mount Zion as a place where God dwells, Isaiah 8:18

Here am I and the children whom the LORD has given me! We are for signs and wonders in Israel From the LORD of hosts, Who dwells in Mount Zion. Isaiah 8:18

Interestingly, Mount Zion tends to take on different meanings depending on the context in which it was used in the Bible. One of the instances for consideration is (Isaiah 8:18) which suggests that God's throne is on Mount Zion. That is, God dwells in His kingdom, but not in the literal sense of a geographical location here on earth as some may think considering the expression, "dwells in Mount Zion." God is omnipresent without doubt, certainly it would be inconceivable for anyone to assume that the same way in which King David lived in his human headquarters during his reign is what God would have done.

Mount Zion as revealing the Second Advent of Christ, Isaiah 24:23

This apocalyptic verse from the book of Isaiah adds another dimension to the theme of Mount Zion as written in (Isaiah 24:23);

Then the moon will be disgraced And the sun ashamed; For the LORD of hosts will reign On Mount Zion and in Jerusalem And before His elders, gloriously. Isaiah 24:23

It should be noted that the topic of our discussion is Mount Zion, however, in regards to (Isaiah 24:23), it relates to the Second Advent of Christ who would make Jerusalem the capital of His empire, where at His appearance, sun and moon will be insignificant because of the radiance of His (Christ's) glory. Not only that, His faithful followers will bask in this glory including the saints who already slept in Christ (cf. the twenty four elders in Revelation 4:4; 7:11; 14:3).[3] As if to add an icing on the cake, an esteemed theologian astutely captured well the millennial reign of Christ in this context, and concludes; "sun and moon will be confounded when Messiah reigns in Mount Zion and before His ancients [referring to the resurrected OT saints] gloriously."[4] In a way, both reputable theologians agree that 'sun and moon' would be outshone by Christ's glory at His Second Coming, that 'sun and moon' won't be needed because Christ's glory passes them all.

Mount Zion as the Temple in Jerusalem, Psalm 74:1-2

O God, why have You cast us off forever? Why does Your anger smoke against the sheep of Your pasture? 2 Remember Your congregation, which You have purchased of old, The tribe of Your inheritance, which You have redeemed—This Mount Zion where You have dwelt. Psalm 74:1-2

Mount Zion was used specifically to describe the Temple in Jerusalem during an invasion by the Chaldean soldiers

[3] Gleason L. Archer, Contribution on Isaiah, in Charles F. Pfeiffer, (ed.), *The Wycliffe Bible Commentary*, Chicago: Moody Press, 1962, p. 626
[4] Merrill F. Unger, *Unger Bible Handbook, An Essential Guide to Understanding the Bible,* Chicago: Moody Press, 1967, p. 322

who burned down the Temple (Psalm 74:1-2),[5] at a time in history. Unsurprisingly, J. A Motyer relates this invasion to the period 587 BC and the events of *2 Kings chapters 24 and 25.[6]

As presented in the above scripture, (Psalm 74:1-2), 'Mount Zion' should be seen as one of the fundamental terms which describes God's relations to His people, but much as it is a relationship of love He had for them, it does not rule out His wrath when necessary. Suffice to say, that each time the Israelites disobeyed God, He allowed one calamity or the other to befall them. By the way, other key terms in the cited passage left for future discussions include, congregation, purchased and redeemed.

Mount Zion as a spiritual invisible Church, Hebrews 12:22

22 But you have come to Mount Zion and to the city of the living God, the heavenly Jerusalem, to an innumerable company of angels. Hebrews 12:22

God who spoke earlier at Sinai (Exodus 19:16-18) through smoke, fire and lightnings with mountains trembling, typically an awesome presence that the Israelites were begging Moses to appeal to Yahweh on their behalf, is the same God calling from heavenly Jerusalem— (Mount Zion), which is quite anti-typical and total opposite of Mount Sinai's experience. Therefore, it should not come as a surprise when Jamieson et al, aptly described Mount Zion in this circumstance as being "the spiritual

---

[5] William MacDonald, (ed.), *Believer's Bible Commentary*, London: Thomas Nelson Publishers, 1989, p. 662

[6] J. A Motyer, Contribution on The Psalms, Amos in D. A Carson, et al (Consulting eds.), *New Bible Commentary, 21st Century Edition*, Leicester, England: InterVarsity Press, 1994, p. 533

* 2 Kings Chapters 24 and 25 full text can be found in Appendices 2 and 3

invisible Church whose foundation was first laid in literal Zion."[7]

One more thing, Merrill Unger, a respectable theologian postulated that it is "grace under the new covenant that brings Hebrew believers to Mount Zion, the city of the Living God, the New Jerusalem, in contrast to the earthly Jerusalem and the fearful Mount Sinai."[8] For me, Mount Zion in the spiritual sense has more eternal value and significance and should be more preferable to a physical site. However, we need the latter (physical site) in order to share a bit of possible human experience. Most important of all, through God's grace we all can come to the true Mount Zion— to the city of the living God, the heavenly Jerusalem where there are numberless company of angels.

* Thank God for the opportunity to learn about Mount Zion (Mount Sion), sing songs of praise and adoration to Him and look forward to His miracles happening in your life soonest. Remember to share the testimony of God's goodness at all times. God bless you.

---

[7] Jamieson, Fausset and Brown, *Commentary On The Whole Bible*, Grand Rapids, Michigan: Zondervan Publishing House, 1961, p. 1440
[8] Merrill F. Unger, *Unger Bible Handbook, An Essential Guide to Understanding the Bible,* Chicago: Moody Press, 1967, p. 777

SECTION EIGHT

THE UPPER ROOM

12 Then they returned to Jerusalem from the mount called Olivet, which is near Jerusalem, a Sabbath day's journey. 13 And when they had entered, they went up into <u>the upper room where they were staying</u>: Peter, James, John, and Andrew; Philip and Thomas; Bartholomew and Matthew; James the son of Alphaeus and Simon the Zealot; and Judas the son of James. 14 These all continued with one accord in prayer and supplication, with the women and Mary the mother of Jesus, and with His brothers. Acts 1:12-14

One of the holy sites which inspires me a lot is the Upper Room in Mount Zion (Mount Sion) in Jerusalem. The place is outside the Old City walls and it is believed to be the site for three different but fundamental events according to Christian tradition. The Upper Room is also known as The Cenacle and is above the building where King David's tomb is situated. The three significant and memorable events which took place at the Upper room are explained below and some prayer points are provided.

The Last Supper

Firstly, it was at the Upper room that Jesus had the Last Supper, washed the feet of His disciples (John 13:1-7, 12-17), and proceeded from there to the Garden of Gethsemane where He often went to pray, (John18:1-2).

Now before the Feast of the Passover, when Jesus knew that His hour had come that He should depart from this world to the Father, having loved His own who were in the world, He loved them to the end. 2 And supper being ended, the devil having already put it into the heart of Judas Iscariot, Simon's son, to betray Him, 3 Jesus, knowing that the Father had given all things into His hands, and that He had come from God and was going to God, 4 rose from supper and laid aside His garments, took a towel and girded Himself. 5 After that, He poured water into a basin and began to wash the disciples' feet, and to wipe them with the towel with which He was girded. 6 Then He came to Simon Peter. And Peter said to Him, "Lord, are You washing my feet?" 7 Jesus answered and said to him, "What I am doing you do not understand now, but you will know after this."

12 So when He had washed their feet, taken His garments, and sat down again, He said to them, "Do you know what I have done to you? 13 You call Me Teacher and Lord, and you say well, for so I am. 14 If I then, your Lord and Teacher, have washed your feet, you also ought to wash one another's feet. 15 For I have given you an example, that you should do as I have done to you. 16 Most assuredly, I say to you, a servant is not greater than his master; nor is he who is sent greater than he who sent him. 17 If you know these things, blessed are you if you do them. John 13:1-7, 12-17

18 When Jesus had spoken these words, He went out with His disciples over the Brook Kidron, where there was a garden, which He and His disciples entered. 2 And Judas, who betrayed Him, also knew the place; for Jesus often met there with His disciples. John18:1-2

What is the significance of the washing of the feet?

As believers we receive once-for all regeneration bath when we confess Christ as our personal Lord and Saviour, but we need continual washing of 'our feet' in the sense that we become defiled as we go out for our daily activities in a sinful world (1 John 1:8-9).[9] Hence, we need to offer prayers of forgiveness of our sins to God from time to time as Jesus taught His disciples to pray (Matthew 6:9-13).

> 8 If we say that we have no sin, we deceive ourselves, and the truth is not in us. 9 If we confess our sins, He is faithful and just to forgive us our sins and to cleanse us from all unrighteousness. 1 John 1:8-9

> 9 In this manner, therefore, pray: Our Father in heaven, Hallowed be Your name. 10 Your kingdom come. Your will be done On earth as it is in heaven. 11 Give us this day our daily bread. 12 And forgive us our debts, As we forgive our debtors. 13 And do not lead us into temptation, But deliver us from the evil one. For Yours is the kingdom and the power and the glory forever. Amen. Matthew 6:9-13

As we return to the story about the washing of the feet of the disciples, Jesus took upon Himself to do the ignoble job which a servant ought to do when guests arrived homes in Palestine. He used this premise to teach His followers a lesson about humility and even for today's disciples of Jesus Christ. As an eminent theologian concluded, the washing of feet "was clearly

---

[9] Merrill Unger, *Unger's Bible Handbook, An Essential Guide to Understanding the Bible*, Chicago: Moody Press, 1967, p. 558

intended to be a symbolic act, symbolic both of cleansing and of humble service" which Jesus' disciples must go ahead and discharge wherever they find themselves in life.[10]

Enter Your Prayer Chamber

Lord my Saviour, from today please order my steps the way I should go:

— In my business
— In my ministry
— In raising all my children
— In my finances
— In all aspects of my life in the name of Jesus Christ

By divine decree my Father, from today let my feet connect with my path of destiny for my good in the name of Jesus Christ

— Father, don't let my feet slip in my path of destiny (repeat 7x)
— O God, don't let my feet slip on the platform of my destiny (repeat 7x)
— Father, don't let me fumble on the platform of my destiny (repeat 7x)
— Almighty Father, don't let me struggle on the platform of my destiny (repeat 7x)

God Almighty, guide my feet towards my mark of greatness

— Guide my feet O Lord (repeat 7x) in the name of Jesus Christ

---

[10] Donald Guthrie, Contribution on John, The Pastoral Letters in D. A Carson, et al, *New Bible Commentary, 21st Century Edition*, Leicester, England: Inter-Varsity Press, 1994, p. 1053

Almighty Father, guide my feet towards my mark of success

— Guide my feet O Lord (repeat 7x) in the name of Jesus Christ

Almighty Father, guide my feet towards my mark of enlargement

— Guide my feet O Lord (repeat 7x) in the name of Jesus Christ

Almighty God, guide my feet towards my mark of promotion

— Guide my feet O Lord (repeat 7x) in the name of Jesus Christ

The Lord of hosts, guide my feet towards my mark of breakthroughs

— Guide my feet O Lord (repeat 7x) in the name of Jesus Christ

Rock of Ages, guide my feet towards my mark of destiny-fulfilment

— Guide my feet O Lord (repeat 7x) in the name of Jesus Christ

Post-Resurrection Appearance

The second reason which makes Upper Room a peculiar holy site is that the post-resurrection appearance of Jesus Christ took place there (John 20:19-23; Luke 24:36-43). This also marked the point where the apostles were commissioned (John 20:21-23).

19 Then, the same day at evening, being the first day of the week, when the doors were shut where the disciples were assembled, for fear of the Jews,

Jesus came and stood in the midst, and said to them, "Peace be with you." 20 When He had said this, He showed them His hands and His side. Then the disciples were glad when they saw the Lord. 21 So Jesus said to them again, "Peace to you! As the Father has sent Me, I also send you." 22 And when He had said this, He breathed on them, and said to them, "Receive the Holy Spirit. 23 If you forgive the sins of any, they are forgiven them; if you retain the sins of any, they are retained." John 20:19-23

The above post-resurrection experience text comes with an additional dimension of what can be called a Pre-Pentecost experience (verse 22 in particular). Jesus' appearance after the resurrection took place on what seems like on a Sunday evening and He breathed on them. However, soon the Holy Spirit will symbolically settle on their heads in Acts 2. Typically, much as the breathing on them has to do with their commission or 'sending to the mission field,' the preceding greeting (Peace to you), must not be overlooked. At the time, the disciples were fearful of their persecutors and discouraged after the crucifixion of their Master (Jesus). Undoubtedly, they needed to be encouraged and their fears to be allayed, hence the greeting. Being the case, the greeting or salutation should not come as a surprise to us— like them, we need hope, courage, faith, encouragement, resilience and so on, as we embark on our daily Christian journey.

Enter Your Prayer Chamber

Jesus appeared to the disciples when they least expected, pray like this:

Master Jesus, appear suddenly and deliver me from all my persecutors

— Appear and deliver me from all my fears O Lord
— Appear and deliver me from the hands of all destiny destroyers Lord Jesus
— Lord Jesus, appear and deliver me from the hands of all marriage destroyers my Saviour
— Appear and deliver me from the hands of all business destroyers, Jesus my Deliverer
— Appear and deliver me Father, from the hands of all ministry destroyers in the name of Jesus Christ.

Jesus acted independently and unhindered even though all doors were shut because of the fear of the Jews as we saw in the post-resurrection appearance, pray like this:

Lord Jesus, suspend natural laws for my sake and grant me unusual miracles from today

Saviour and Lord Jesus, suspend natural laws for my sake and grant me access to my higher grounds

Master Jesus, suspend natural laws for my sake and grant me unusual mercy and favour

Lord Jesus, suspend natural laws for my sake and shower me with incomparable goodness

Thou Son of David, suspend natural laws for my sake and let me enjoy open-heaven prosperity from today

Thou Son of David, suspend natural laws for my sake and remove suddenly every diabolical barrier working against my life

Thou Son of David, suspend natural laws for my sake and remove immediately every socio-political opposition working against my family

Lord Jesus, suspend natural laws for my sake and remove by force every evil institution working against me and my spouse

Lord Jesus, suspend natural laws for my sake and remove every satanic collaborators working against me and my children

Thou Risen Lord, suspend natural laws for my sake and remove by fire every barrier working against my business

Risen Lord, suspend natural laws for my sake and remove by thunder every barrier working against me and my ministry

Risen Lord, suspend natural laws for my sake and remove now every barrier working against my finances

Lord Jesus, suspend natural laws for my sake and remove forthwith every barrier working against my health, amen!

The Coming of the Holy Spirit

The third reason that makes Upper Room to be a significant holy site is that, the coming of the Holy Spirit on the Day of Pentecost happened there (Acts 2:1-4). This marks the beginning of the Church as the Body of Christ came to be known. Also, it confirms the outpouring of the Spirit which was prophesied in (Joel 2:28). Through the outpouring of the Spirit on that day at the Upper Room, it is evidently clear that Christianity is not limited to any particular race, nationality, language or group of people. Till today, a lot of Christian believers all over the world go to this holy site and many others in The Holy Land.

2 When the Day of Pentecost had fully come, they were all with one accord in one place. 2 And suddenly there came a sound from heaven, as of a rushing mighty wind, and it filled the whole house where they were sitting. 3 Then there appeared to them divided tongues, as of fire, and one sat upon each of them. 4 And they were all filled with the Holy Spirit and began to speak with other tongues, as the Spirit gave them utterance. Acts 2:1-4

Enter Your Prayer Chamber

(Please sing this song by Paul Armstrong[11] if you know it before you start to pray).

> Spirit of the living God
> Fall afresh on me
> Fill me anew
> Fill me anew
> Spirit of the Lord
> Fall afresh on me

My Father and my God, please fill me anew with your Holy Spirit to enable me to do your will all the days of my life

— Fill me anew O God (repeat 7x) in the name of Jesus Christ

Lord, fill me afresh with your Holy Spirit to enable me remain in your will all the days of my life

— Fill me afresh O God (repeat 7x) in the name of Jesus Christ

God Almighty, fill me anew with your Holy Spirit to prevent me from stumbling in my faith in the name of Jesus Christ

My Father and my God, fill me afresh with your Holy Spirit to disallow me from compromising my faith in you in the name of Jesus Christ

— Lord fill me anew with your Holy Spirit so I can fulfil my destiny assignment the way you intended it for me

---

[11] Paul Armstrong, *Songs of Fellowship — Combined Words Edition,* Eastbourne: Kingsway Music, 2002, Hymn 511

— Lord, make me a worthy carrier of your Holy Spirit all the days of my life
— My Father, make me a worthy custodian of your Holy Spirit all the days of my life in the name of Jesus Christ.

* Thank God for answering your prayers, sing songs of praise and adoration to Him, and look forward to His miracles happening in your life soonest. Remember to share the testimony of God's goodness at all times please. God bless you.

SECTION NINE

THE POOLS OF BETHESDA

This holy site (John 5:1-2) had a Pool with five porches which suggests the name Pools of Bethesda. However, some Bible teachers think the five porches represent the five Books (Law) of Moses namely, Genesis, Exodus, Leviticus, Numbers and Deuteronomy. Can this be true? Further, the commentators argue that the five Books of Moses are not able to help man out of his deep troubles[12] unless Jesus comes to our rescue like the person cited in the below Bible passage (John 5:1-9). Let us read:

> 5 After this there was a feast of the Jews, and Jesus went up to Jerusalem. 2 Now there is in Jerusalem by the Sheep Gate a pool, which is called in Hebrew, Bethesda, having five porches. 3 In these lay a great multitude of sick people, blind, lame, paralyzed, waiting for the moving of the water. 4 For an angel went down at a certain time into the pool and stirred up the water; then whoever stepped in first, after the stirring of the water, was made well of whatever disease he had. 5 Now a certain man was there who had an infirmity thirty-eight years. 6 When Jesus saw him lying there, and knew that he already had been in that condition a long time, He said to him, "Do you want to be made well?" 7 The sick man answered Him, "Sir, I have no man to put me into the pool when the water is stirred up; but while I am

---

[12] William MacDonald, (Art Farstad, ed.), *Believer's Bible Commentary,* London: Thomas Nelson Publishers, 1995, p. 1490

coming, another steps down before me." 8 Jesus said to him, "Rise, take up your bed and walk." 9 And immediately the man was made well, took up his bed, and walked ... John 5:1-9

Bethesda which has been described as house of grace[13] and another writer calls it the house of mercy or house of pity,[14] was a colony filled with invalids crowded around the unsheltered Pool awaiting their healing. However, there were conditions that the invalids had to meet for their healing miracles to happen. According to the biblical account, it used to be an annual occurrence when the Pool was stirred by an angel, and any person desirous of healing had to enter quickly. We are not too sure if some were permanently resident there or commuted occasionally. Regrettably, nobody knew when the angel would come for the stirring of the medicinal water. Another probable challenge for the invalids was that, the individual must be ready to jump in first, it is the one who jumped into the Pool first that would receive healing miracle.

It was quite unfortunate, but not surprising that a person missed thirty eight chances, each opportunity missed meant a year wait— the competition was strong. Unexpectedly, Jesus came there on a particular day and asked the man, "Do you want to be made well?" Don't let us get it wrong, the question which was asked by Jesus was a loving and compassion-filled one, but some people might not see it that way. Indeed, it was a question from a Compassionate God. As I think, stating that this man had been ill for thirty eight years shows that God keeps account of how long we have been suffering from one thing or the other— we can be comforted and hopeful

---

[13] Merrill Unger, *Unger's Bible Handbook, An Essential Guide to Understanding the Bible*, Chicago: Moody Press, 1967, p. 550

[14] William MacDonald, (Art Farstad, ed.), *Believer's Bible Commentary*, London: Thomas Nelson Publishers, 1995, p.1490

from this helpless man's experience. Certainly, he never expected help at the time when it came through the Man of Galilee.

Enter Your Prayer Chamber

The sick man desired to be healed but lacked the means, but Jesus provided the means. Pray like this:

Lord Jesus, please grant me the necessary access to my miracles from today in your Precious Name

— Grant me access Jehovah (repeat 7x) in the name of Jesus Christ

Lord Jesus, through your help please usher me into the realm of my miracles in your Precious Name

— I command miracles of healing to fall on me in the name of Jesus Christ
— I declare miracles of victory upon me and my family in the name of Jesus Christ
— Miracles of breakthrough! fall upon my business without delay in the name of Jesus Christ
— Miracles that will transform my entire ministry! descend on me from this moment in the name of Jesus Christ.

Lord Almighty, please provide me with the means that will take me out of every deep troubles in the name of Jesus Christ

— Provide it today my Father in the name of Jesus Christ

The story teaches us that people can miss their season, pray like this:

My ordained seasons of miracles! Return to me in the name of Jesus Christ

— Return to me (repeat 7x) in the name of Jesus Christ

Out of the multitudes in the colonnade, Jesus walked to that man. Pray like this:

My Father, let your distinguishing grace fall upon me and my spouse from today

- My Father and my God, let your distinguishing grace fall upon me and my children from today in the name of Jesus Christ
- Lord Jesus, let your distinguishing grace locate me and my entire family from today
- Gracious Father, let your distinguishing grace turn my life and business around from today in the name of Jesus Christ
- Almighty Father, let your distinguishing grace turn my life and ministry around from today in the name of Jesus Christ.

Lord Jesus, please crush into pieces all my hopeless situation and grant me new opportunities

- Grant me new opportunities Father (repeat 7x) in the name of Jesus Christ

From today, my Compassionate Saviour, please crush into pieces all my helpless situation and let me leap for joy instantly in the name of Jesus Christ of Nazareth.

* Thank God for answering your prayers, sing songs of praise and adoration to Him, and look forward to His miracles happening in your life soonest. Remember to share the testimony of God's goodness at all times please. God bless you.

SECTION TEN

TABGHA MENSA CHRISTI

THE MULTIPLICATION OF LOAVES AND FISHES

Bible Texts: John 6:5-13; Matthew 14: 14-21; Luke 9:10-17

The miracle of the multiplication of loaves and fishes took place at this site— Tabgha Mensa Christi. Christ Jesus provided strength and energy that the immediate audience required through the loaves and fishes which were eaten at the site. But first, a lad committed to Jesus' hands at that time the loaves and the fishes he (the lad) had, Jesus is still willing to do miracles today if we can put our trust in Him. Note this, our limited resources can go places when we trustingly hand over our 'little' resources to Him. All we need to remember is, He has the capacity to multiply what we give to Him and make it become more than enough (John 6:5-13). Why not be the 'lad' for the moment?

5 Then Jesus lifted up His eyes, and seeing a great multitude coming toward Him, He said to Philip, "Where shall we buy bread, that these may eat?" 6 But this He said to test him, for He Himself knew what He would do. 7 Philip answered Him, "Two hundred denarii worth of bread is not sufficient for them, that every one of them may have a little." 8 One of His disciples, Andrew, Simon Peter's brother, said to Him, 9 "There is a lad here who has

five barley loaves and two small fish, but what are they among so many?" 10 Then Jesus said, "Make the people sit down." Now there was much grass in the place. So the men sat down, in number about five thousand. 11 And Jesus took the loaves, and when He had given thanks He distributed them to the disciples, and the disciples to those sitting down; and likewise of the fish, as much as they wanted. 12 So when they were filled, He said to His disciples, "Gather up the fragments that remain, so that nothing is lost." 13 Therefore they gathered them up, and filled twelve baskets with the fragments of the five barley loaves which were left over by those who had eaten. John 6:5-13

As could be seen in the above narration, it does not matter who gave away the loaves of bread and the pieces of fish— young, old, male or female. Do you know God wants to distribute what His children bring to Him like the days at Tabgha? Have you got something to give to kick-start God's moment of miracles? Yes, you do. Like the wife of the prophet in (2 Kings 4:2) you might have a little oil in your jar at home to spare, or some skills set, gifts, other resources and so on.

2 So Elisha said to her, "What shall I do for you? Tell me, what do you have in the house?" And she said, "Your maidservant has nothing in the house but a jar of oil." 2 Kings 4:2.

Enter Your Prayer Chamber

The power that multiplied the loaves and the fishes!

— Grant me the provision that will advance God's kingdom from today in the name of Jesus Christ
— Give me the provision that will advance my life and family from today in the name of Jesus Christ

- Release the provision that will advance my business from today in the name of Jesus Christ
- Provide the provision that will advance my ministry from today in the name of Jesus Christ
- Produce the provision that will advance my career from today in the name of Jesus Christ
- Multiply my 'loaves and fishes' my Father and grant me testimonies right now in the name of Jesus Christ of Nazareth
- Multiply my 'loaves and fishes' Jehovah (repeat 7x) in the name of Jesus Christ

The power that multiplied the loaves and the fishes, treat my case with the urgency required in the name of Jesus Christ

- The power that multiplied the loaves and the fishes be my portion in the name of Jesus Christ

The power that multiplied the loaves and the fishes, do miracles in my life in the name of Jesus Christ
The power that multiplied the loaves and the fishes, let God's name be glorified in my life in the name of Jesus Christ
The power that multiplied the loaves and the fishes, treat my case favourably in the name of Jesus Christ

- Lord, let people join me to praise your name because of me (repeat 7x)

The power that multiplied the loaves and the fishes, provide for all my lack from today in the name of Jesus Christ

- Lord, provide for all my lack financially, materially and vocationally
- Jehovah Jireh, provide for all the needs of my family and ministry
- My Father, provide for all the needs associated with my project in the name of Jesus Christ

As we read in the narration, the young lad was kind and he gave his five barley loaves and two small fish sacrificially. He is famous and is known all over the world till today. Pray like this:

My Father show me what to do to become famous in the name of Jesus Christ

- Show my spouse what to do in the name of Jesus Christ
- Show my children what to do in the name of Jesus Christ
- Show my entire family what to do in the name of Jesus Christ

My Father, show me what to do that would let my business become famous

- Show me Lord (repeat 7x) in the name of Jesus Christ

Jesus of Nazareth, show me what to do that would let my ministry become famous

- Show me Lord (repeat 7x) in the name of Jesus Christ

Obviously the young lad was very kind, an ambassador worth emulating. Pray like this:

Father, bless me and make me an ambassador of kindness, globally and generationally in the name of Jesus Christ

Frankly, nobody can explain how the loaves and the fishes multiplied. Pray like this:

My God and my Father, please grant me miracles that defy human explanations —

— Medically
— Physically
— Vocationally
— Academically
— Financially
— And in every way that would glorify your name in the name of Jesus Christ.

An instruction was given to the disciples to gather the leftovers after the multitudes finished eating. This suggests that God does not want us to waste His bounties or His provision especially, when we thought that we got them for free. Pray like this:

Lord my Father, help me to be accountable in my entrusted field in the name of Jesus Christ
Lord Jesus, please don't let me be a waster of your resources in the name of Jesus Christ
Lord Jesus, help me to be a good steward of your blessings in my life in the name of Jesus Christ

— Father, let my family be a good steward of your blessings in the name of Jesus Christ
— Jehovah, let my ministry be a good steward of your blessings in the name of Jesus Christ
— God Almighty, let my business be a good steward of your blessings in the name of Jesus Christ of Nazareth.

* Thank God for answering your prayers, sing songs of praise and adoration to Him, and look forward to His miracles happening in your life soonest. Remember to share the testimony of God's goodness at all times, God bless you.

SECTION ELEVEN

CANA OF GALILEE

THE SUPERNATURAL WINE DISTILLERY

According to the Bible, this was where Jesus of Nazareth performed His first miracle by turning water into wine. The supernatural wine distillery process was so abrupt and extraordinary that the Governor of the wedding had to interrogate the bridegroom about reserving the best wine till that moment. The Governor never knew about the source which the wine came from. What people should notice is that tradition, and popular beliefs, personal opinions or philosophy can never stand in the way of God when He is ready to move or cause miracles to come about (John 2:1-11). Like the original celebrants in the story, it is wise to invite Jesus to your events (as true believers), because you never know what could happen in the next minute. Not only your events, but determine that your life, home, business, ministry and so on, should be a place you wish Him (Jesus) to share with you. Please read the Bible text:

On the third day there was a wedding in Cana of Galilee, and the mother of Jesus was there. 2 Now both Jesus and His disciples were invited to the wedding. 3 And when they ran out of wine, the mother of Jesus said to Him, "They have no wine." 4 Jesus said to her, "Woman, what does your concern have to do with Me? My hour has not yet come." 5 His mother said to the servants, "Whatever He says to you, do it." 6 Now there were set there six waterpots of stone, according to the manner of purification of the Jews, containing twenty or thirty gallons apiece. 7 Jesus said to them, "Fill the waterpots with water." And they filled them up to the brim. 8 And He said to them, "Draw some out now, and take it to the master of the feast." And they took it. 9 When the master of the feast had tasted the water that was made wine, and did not know where it came from (but the servants who had drawn the water knew), the master of the feast called the bridegroom. 10 And he said to him, "Every man at the beginning sets out the good wine, and when the guests have well drunk, then the inferior. You have kept the good wine until now!" 11 This beginning of signs Jesus did in Cana of Galilee, and manifested His glory; and His disciples believed in Him. John 2:1-11

One of the most essential items for the occasion was wine. For the ceremony, wine is supposed to bring joy and lift the mood of the participants as they rejoice with the bride and the bridegroom. It could have been embarrassing to run out of wine during the celebration. We do not know how many days it was into the wedding celebration, but according to Jewish tradition it was supposed to be a week-long festivity.

However, thank God for the likes of Donald Guthrie who concluded that, the followers of Christ more than the general onlookers saw the richness of new life in Christ Jesus when he turned the water into sweet wine.[15] Without contention, the issue about whether it was alcoholic or a non-alcoholic wine is beyond the scope of

---

[15] Donald Guthrie, Contribution on John and The Pastoral Letters in D. A Carson, et al, (Consulting eds.), *New Bible Commentary, 21st Century Edition*, Leicester, England: Inter-Varsity Press, 1994, p. 1030

this book. Let us turn our attention to Jesus' response to Mary the earthly mother.

Jesus' response to the earthly mother that, "Woman, what does your concern have to do with Me? My hour has not yet come," should not be taken out of context. For the purposes of clarity, "Woman" as used in the text was a title of respect as we use "lady" to address a female person today. Jesus was not harsh, cold, rude or insultive. Mary understood Jesus hence, she said, "Whatever He says to you, do it." On Jesus' part, He was indicating how His divine mission was led by His Father in heaven, and He (Jesus), had to act in obedience to God— His Father. It was important for Jesus to emphasise that He was not subject to (Mary) His mother's instruction for His assignment.[16] One of the big lessons for us here is that, we should allow God to guide us, lead us and trust Him as we take important decisions in our lives. In any case, it remains unchanged that Jesus turned water into wine in Cana of Galilee so that a soothing and a memorable wedding celebration could be enjoyed (John 2:8).

Enter Your Prayer Chamber

In his description, Unger said, "the wine is typical of the joy and ministration of grace which Jesus came to bring, … the Creator alone is the One who can Re-create," therefore let us ask Him to re-create whatever that is missing as you pray:

— My Father, please re-create all that is needed for my marriage to flourish
— Gracious Father, re-create all that is required for my family to flourish
— Almighty Father, re-create all that is necessary for my ministry to flourish

---

[16] William MacDonald, (Art Farstad, ed.), *Believer's Bible Commentary*, London: Thomas Nelson Publishers, 1995, pp. 1473-1474

- Glorious Father, re-create all that is needful for my business to flourish
- All-powerful Father, re-create all that is necessary for my entire endeavours to flourish in the name of Jesus Christ.

The miracle turned a potential bad and embarrassing situation around for the better for the bride, bridegroom and their families, pray like this:

- Every bad and possible embarrassing situation around my life, reverse now in the name of Jesus Christ
- Every potential bad and embarrassing situation around my family, reverse now in the name of Jesus Christ
- Every conceivable bad and embarrassing situation around my ministry, reverse now and terminate yourself forever in the name of Jesus Christ
- Terminate yourself forever in the name of Jesus Christ (repeat 7x)
- Every bad and likely embarrassing situation around my business, be roasted by fire and burn beyond repair in the name of Jesus Christ.
- Burn beyond repair in the name of Jesus Christ (repeat 7x)

The disastrous end that could have broken the unwritten code of hospitality was reversed when Jesus turned the water into sweet wine, pray like this:

- Omnipotent Father! Reverse all disastrous situations (medical, financial, economic, court case, vocational, etc.,), for me from today in the name of Jesus Christ

The disgraceful conclusion that could have broken the unwritten code of hospitality was reversed when Jesus turned the water into sweet wine, pray like this:

— Almighty Father! Reverse all disgraceful situations (marital, ministry assignment, career, etc.,), for the better for me from today in the name of Jesus Christ

Turning water into sweet wine simply demonstrated God's power, pray like this:

Omnipotent God, please demonstrate your power openly in my entire life from today in the name of Jesus Christ

— Great Father, demonstrate your power openly for me (repeat 7x) in the name of Jesus Christ

Omniscient Father, demonstrate your power publicly throughout my whole life for the sake of your glory, from today in the name of Jesus Christ
Omnipotent God, demonstrate your power directly into my entire life for the sake of your name, from today in the name of Jesus Christ

* Thank God for answering your prayers, sing songs of praise and adoration to Him, and look forward to His miracles happening in your life soonest. Remember to share the testimony of God's goodness at all times, God bless you.

SECTION TWELVE

MOUNT TABOR

THE MOUNT OF TRANSFIGURATION

As a Christian believer, I encourage every person who go on spiritual pilgrimage to The Holy Land to ensure they visit this holy site. It is a place I call three-in-one site. It was here that the missions of Moses, Elijah and Jesus of Nazareth were unified (Luke 9:28-36; Matthew 17:1-9; Mark 9:2-10). One of the common denominators between Moses and Elijah was rejection and suffering during their God-given assignment. However, due to Jesus' Messianic role, He too would soon experience suffering, rejection and death in Jerusalem.[17]

28 Now it came to pass, about eight days after these sayings, that He took Peter, John, and James and went up on the mountain to pray. 29 As He prayed, the appearance of His face was altered, and His robe became white and glistening. 30 And behold, two men talked with Him, who were Moses and Elijah, 31 who appeared in glory and spoke of His decease which He was about to accomplish at Jerusalem. 32 But Peter and those with him were heavy with sleep; and when they were fully awake, they saw His glory and the two men who stood with Him. 33 Then it happened, as they were parting

---

[17] R. T France, Commentary on Matthew, in Leon Morris, (General ed.), *Tyndale New Testament Commentaries*, Leicester, England: Inter-Varsity Press, 1985, p. 263

from Him, that Peter said to Jesus, "Master, it is good for us to be here; and let us make three tabernacles: one for You, one for Moses, and one for Elijah"—not knowing what he said. 34 While he was saying this, a cloud came and overshadowed them; and they were fearful as they entered the cloud. 35 And a voice came out of the cloud, saying, "This is My beloved Son. Hear Him!" 36 When the voice had ceased, Jesus was found alone. But they kept quiet, and told no one in those days any of the things they had seen. Luke 9:28-36

Before we go too far, it should be noted that Jesus' transfiguration provides a glimpse of His glory in which He will return for His Second Advent to judge the whole world.[18] Assuredly, God who owns Jesus and accepts Him as His beloved Son, is ready to accept us through the Saviour of the world— Jesus of Nazareth. Without doubt, the unification which took place on this mountain is very important for today's believers for various reasons. For example, it highlights the significance of the Old Testament (OT) as being the platform on which God started most of what would happen in the New Testament (NT). In the most simplest way to explain it, imagine a building facility without a foundation, (suspended in the air?), how secure do you think the structure would be? No building is built without sitting on a foundation, the Old Testament is like the foundation on which God started to build 'the house' which today we can call the New Testament. So, the two Testaments— both the Old and New Testaments are inseparable. The stories about Moses and Elijah would be found in the Old Testament but the Messiah was predicted there too, (a few example include, Isaiah 9:6-7, 53:1-12; Zechariah 9:9-10; Micah 5:2-5,

---

[18] *Matthew Henry's Commentary on The Whole Bible*, Chicago, Illinois: Operation Mobilization Literature, 1995, p. 752

cf. Luke 2:4-6). However, when the Messiah eventually arrived, His stories have been presented to us in the New Testament. For short, the stories are interlinked.

Each of the three representatives who met on this mountain namely, Moses, Elijah and Jesus Christ is a key player to our religious practice. Moses not only reminds us about the Law but he was the bearer of it, the one who was commissioned for the exodus of God's people from the land of Egypt to the Promised Land (Exodus 3: 7-8). For Kingdom worship to return to Israel again, God brought Elijah to confront the authorities of the time, particularly during the reign of Ahab (1 Kings 16:33). Typically, on Mount Carmel, Elijah was the prophet of God who brought the people back from their idolatrous worship of Baal to return to Yahweh, the Only One who is the true God as they exclaimed after they saw fire fell from heaven, "The LORD, He is God! (1 Kings 18:38-39).

7 And the LORD said: "I have surely seen the oppression of My people who are in Egypt, and have heard their cry because of their taskmasters, for I know their sorrows. 8 So I have come down to deliver them out of the hand of the Egyptians, and to bring them up from that land to a good and large land, to a land flowing with milk and honey, to the place of the Canaanites and the Hittites and the Amorites and the Perizzites and the Hivites and the Jebusites. Exodus 3:7-8

33 And Ahab made a wooden image. Ahab did more to provoke the LORD God of Israel to anger than all the kings of Israel who were before him. 1 Kings 16:33

38 Then the fire of the LORD fell and consumed the burnt sacrifice, and the wood and the stones and the dust, and it licked up the water that was in the trench. 39 Now when all the people saw it, they fell

on their faces; and they said, "The LORD, He is God!
The LORD, He is God!" 1 Kings 18:38-39

We should remember that we are part of the 'Exodus'—
one time or the other, called from utter darkness to God's
marvellous light, He turned us to Kingdom citizens with a
circumcised heart, and made us ready to be part of the
new birth in Christ Jesus. As Leon Morris concluded, "the
exodus had delivered Israel from bondage (in Egypt), so
Jesus by His 'exodus' would deliver His people from a far
worse bondage."[19] Also, on this mountain we are called to
partake in the glow, glory and radiance of Jesus' appearance
bequeathed to us when it happened on that day to the Man
of Galilee on the Mount of Transfiguration.

But we must have the heart of faith and hope.
Importantly, be ready to be part of the suffering and death
of Christ Jesus so that in the end, we can fully partake of
His victory and the blessedness of the resurrection. The
Master already told us, we are in the world, but not of the
world (John17:15-16).

15 I do not pray that You should take them out of
the world, but that You should keep them from the
evil one. 16 They are not of the world, just as I am
not of the world. John17:15-16

As Jesus wasn't afraid to leave this world, so we shouldn't.
Being the case, we should not be surprised that after the
discussion among the trio about the imminent persecution
and death which was to take place in Jerusalem, the Law
bearer (Moses) and Elijah representing the Prophets
departed, thus the unification was consummated. As
Jesus returned to His duties at Jerusalem so we all have

---

[19] Leon Morris, (General ed.), *Luke - Tyndale New Testament
Commentaries,* Leicester, England: Inter-Varsity Press, 1999, p. 189

to return to our 'Jerusalem' in our Christian journey. We can be of good cheer because our Master has led the way.

Enter Your Prayer Chamber

The cloud that overshadowed them was an emblem of the Divine presence and glory.[20] Pray like this:

My Father and my God from today, let your Divine presence overshadow me all the days of my life

— Let your Divine presence overshadow my entire family in the name of Jesus Christ

My Father and my God from today, let your Divine presence accompany me wherever I go in the name of Jesus Christ

— Let your Divine presence accompany me in the name of Jesus Christ

My Father, envelope me with your Divine presence all the days of my life

— Let your Divine presence envelope me in the name of Jesus Christ

Omnipresent God, allow me and my entire family to experience and enjoy your Divine presence all the days of our lives in the name of Jesus Christ

And a voice came out of the cloud, saying, "This is My beloved Son. Hear Him!" Luke 9:35

— Father, in the name of Jesus Christ, let your anointing for Divine endorsement rest upon my life from today

---

[20] *Matthew Henry's Commentary on The Whole Bible*, Chicago, Illinois: Operation Mobilization Literature, 1995, p. 701

- Rest upon me (repeat 7x) in the name of Jesus Christ
- Anointing for Divine endorsement rest upon my life (repeat 7x)
- Anointing for Divine endorsement rest upon my family (repeat 7x)
- Anointing for Divine endorsement rest upon my ministry [Name it] (repeat 7x)
- Anointing for Divine endorsement rest upon my vocation (repeat 7x)
- Anointing for Divine endorsement rest upon all my endeavours (repeat 7x) in the name of Jesus Christ

Council of Heaven, arrange a meeting in my favour in the name of Jesus Christ

- Meeting of blessing and prosperity
- Meeting of good health and longevity
- Meeting of successful accomplishments all round
- Meeting of victory and Joy
- Meeting of peace and rest of mind in the name of Jesus Christ

God of Moses, God of Elijah and Jesus Christ, the Saviour of mankind—

- Defend my life
- Protect my glory
- Guard my destiny
- Keep all my biological and spiritual family safe wherever they are
- Protect my spouse and all my children
- Defend all my destiny-helpers in the name of Jesus Christ

Moses was distinguished during his time in ministry, Almighty Father, let me outshine all my competitors in the name of Jesus Christ

- Let all my family members outshine their competitors

God of Elijah! Put to shame all antagonists challenging my calling

- — Put to shame all adversaries challenging my ministry
- — Put to shame all opponents challenging my marriage
- — Put to shame all opposition challenging my career
- — Put to shame all adversaries challenging my glory
- — Put to shame all opponents challenging my life in the name of Jesu Christ

Thank God for answering your prayers, give praises and adoration to Him, Amen.

SECTION THIRTEEN

THE TOMB OF LAZARUS

POWER OF DEATH DESTROYED

In most cultures people have different explanations about the dead coming back to life again. The cultural beliefs and oral traditions have crept into other human disciplines and thereby shaped, or taint how people view things, or events. However, in the story about Lazarus being raised from death to life, we shall keep to the biblical narration as provided in (John 11:1-44). It is a long read (See Appendix 4), but would help to produce the comprehensive detail necessary to deepen one's understanding about what really happened and how everything unfolded over the four days of it occurring. Let us remember that Jesus had claimed that He has divine power to bestow eternal life upon anyone who is spiritually dead, but raising Lazarus who had died physically for four days is a different matter. Of course, Jesus used His divine power to raise others back to life such as, Jairus daughter in (Mark 5:22-43) and the son of the widow at Nain (Luke 7:11-17).

The scripture make us to understand that the disciples were concerned about Jesus' safety when they were told they would return to Judea (Bethany) where Lazarus was pronounced dead. The reason was because the Jews sought to kill Jesus (John 11:7-8). Although Jesus loved the family, but He waited for another two days before travelling there. One of the probable reasons for the wait was to let us see Him as the resurrection and life. Also, to allow the entire action unfold in a way that would bring glory to God the Father. Another point to note is that, so that the disciples' faith in Jesus Christ as the Giver of life would increase when practically they see Him raise a man from an obvious corruption to incorruption.[21] Without wasting time, Jesus called Lazarus to come forth because His (Jesus) voice was life-giving, and the One who called the world into existence, spoke life into a dead man and His words went forth into that dead situation with power and the result was obvious for everyone to see. God's word is power-packed— It is the Word of life![22]

Enter Your Prayer Chamber

Life-giving voice of Jesus descend upon my life and grant me miracles

Power-packed anointing through Jesus' voice descend upon me and my family and grant us miracles

Power-packed anointing from Jesus descend upon my ministry and grant us miracles

Power-packed anointing from Jesus descend upon my business and grant me miracles

Jesus the Giver of life, jump-start all my situation that looks 'dead' and give me testimony in the name of Jesus Christ

- — Jumpstart my life financially
- — Jumpstart my life maritally
- — Jumpstart my career
- — Jumpstart my health and heal me completely in the name of Jesus Christ

[21] R. V. G Tasker, (General ed.), *John, Tyndale New Testament Commentaries,* Leicester, England: Inter-Varsity Press, 1999, p. 139
[22] Marilyn Hickey, *The Gospel of John — Classic Library Edition*, Denver, Colorado: Marilyn Hickey Ministries, 2000, p. 173

The power that turned the situation around for Lazarus and his family, I am available,!

— Release my miracles to me in the name of Jesus Christ (repeat 7x)

The power that turned mourning into dancing for Lazarus and his family, my life is available! Let my miracles locate me in the name of Jesus Christ

— Locate me now (repeat 7x)

And some of them said, "Could not this Man, who opened the eyes of the blind, also have kept this man from dying?" (John 11:37).

The power that mocked the mockers for Lazarus and his family, I am available, let all my mockers be disgraced in the name of Jesus Christ

As a result of the miracle of raising Lazarus back to life from death, they changed the name of Bethany to Azariyeh.[23] Pray like this:

Miracles that will commemorate my name, be my portion in the name of Jesus Christ

Ministry that will memorialise my name, be my portion in the name of Jesus Christ

Business that will immortalise my name, be my portion in the name of Jesus Christ

The news about what happened to Lazarus circulated throughout Bethany, pray like this:

Ground-breaking news that will make people serve God with me, come and be my portion in the name of Jesus Christ

---

[23] Marilyn Hickey, *The Gospel of John — Classic Library Edition*, Denver, Colorado: Marilyn Hickey Ministries, 2000, p. 173

Ear-tinkling testimonies be my portion from now in the name of Jesus Christ

Ear-tinkling testimonies be my family's portion from now in the name of Jesus Christ

Ear-tinkling testimonies be my spouse's portion from now in the name of Jesus Christ

Ear-tinkling testimonies be my business' portion from now in the name of Jesus Christ

Ear-tinkling testimonies be my ministry's portion from now in the name of Jesus Christ

God who glorified His name over Lazarus' death— glorify your name in my life from today

- — Glorify your name in my marriage
- — Glorify your name in my health
- — Glorify your name in my ministry
- — Glorify your name in my finances
- — Glorify your name in my business
- — Glorify your name in all my endeavours in the name of Jesus Christ

Jesus said, "Take away the stone," (John 11 :39). Pray like this:

Every satanic blockage militating against my progress in ministry and business, hear the voice of the Lord, and be removed in the name of Jesus Christ of Nazareth

- — Be removed (repeat 7x) in the name of Jesus Christ

Every satanic barrier erected against my advancement, roll away by the power of the Invisible Hand of God — Roll away (repeat 7x) in the name of Jesus Christ

Every satanic blockage dictating how far I can go in life, your tenure is over!

- — Terminate in the name of Jesus Christ (repeat 7x)

43 Now when He had said these things, He (Jesus) cried with a loud voice, "Lazarus, come forth!" (John 11:43). Pray like this:

My miracles come forth! and be alive in Jesus name
My breakthroughs come forth! and be alive in Jesus name
My blessings come forth! and be alive in Jesus name
My effectual doors come forth! and be alive in Jesus name
My promotion come forth! and be alive in Jesus name
My enlargements come forth! and be alive in Jesus name
My prosperity come forth! and be alive in Jesus name

44 And he who had died came out bound hand and foot with graveclothes, and his face was wrapped with a cloth. Jesus said to them, "Loose him, and let him go." (John 11:44). Pray like this:

Covenant of death and coffin assigned against me and my family, hear the voice of the Lord and loose your grip in the name of Jesus Christ

— Loose your grip in the name of Jesus Christ (repeat 7x)

Covenant of grave and graveclothes assigned against me and my ministry, loose your power and return back to your sender in the name of Jesus Christ

— Back to your sender in the name of Jesus (repeat 7x)

Covenant of bereavement and graveclothes assigned against me and my business, hear the voice of the Lord and terminate yourself in the name of Jesus Christ

— Terminate yourself in the name of Jesus Christ (repeat 7x)

*Thank God for answering your prayers, sing songs of praise and adoration to Him, and look forward to His miracles happening in your life soonest. Remember to share the testimony of God's goodness at all times, God bless you.

SECTION FOURTEEN

THE HOLY SEPULCHRE

Bible Texts: Matthew 28:1-7; Mark 16:1-7; Luke 24:1-10; John 20:1-18

The Holy Sepulchre was where the tomb of Jesus is purported to be, meaning that it was the place where His body after it was requested by Joseph of Arimathea and prepared, was buried (Matthew 27:57-60). The other place that is suggested as Jesus' tomb is called the Garden Tomb. Personally an unforgettable encounter which I had in one of my spiritual pilgrimages happened at the Holy Sepulchre which remains with me till today. Let us read Matthew 27:57-60,

Now when evening had come, there came a rich man from Arimathea, named Joseph, who himself had also become a disciple of Jesus. 58 This man went to Pilate and asked for the body of Jesus. Then Pilate commanded the body to be given to him. 59 When Joseph had taken the body, he wrapped it in a clean linen cloth, 60 and laid it in his new tomb which he had hewn out of the rock; and he rolled a large stone against the door of the tomb, and departed. Matthew 27:57-60

About ten years ago if someone said to me I would write about this holy site one day, I would not have believed it. But God's ways are not our ways. On a particular day in 2013 at this holy site (The Holy Sepulchre), the Lord spoke so audibly to my ear that out of joy, excitement and answer to my prayers, I felt I should cut short my spiritual pilgrimage and return to London immediately, but I couldn't because we travelled as a group and we had to return as a group. It was an inexpressible encounter. I wish I could share the story but it is a personal one. The only aspect I can mention is that, till date I am in close contact with two of the ministers of God who travelled with our group that year.

Food For Thoughts

As we turn our attention to the story about the Holy Sepulchre, it would be discovered that the Synoptic gospels (Matthew, Mark and Luke) almost told their stories in a similar way, but not really so in the Johanine account (John 20:1-18). John's account contains some remarkable differences. Having said that, Jesus' resurrection from death was never disputed by any of the synoptic gospel writers and John. However each writer or eyewitness wrote what impressed them most. For instance, Matthew records that an angel of the Lord came from heaven, and rolled the stone away from the tomb's entrance and sat on it (Matthew 28:1-7). Fortunately, Marcan account confirms that it was a large stone (Mark16:4). As for Luke, he recorded that there were two men in dazzling clothes (Luke 24:4). In a nutshell, I can say that the synoptic gospel writers and John, expressly narrated that there was a divine intervention in the removal of the stone (Matthew 28:2; Mark 16:4; Luke 24:2 John 20:1).

Also, in their account a physical but at the same time, a divine personality spoke to the human witnesses who were women. On the other hand, the divine agents reminded the women about how Jesus had told them He would rise from the dead on the third day. Let me say this, although the disciples were fearful at that time, but they were loyal. Further, they were faced by unexplainable situation, but God was able to support and saw them through their difficulties. What this means is that, God is the One who dispels our fear and removes our difficulties.

Reference Text: Mark 17:1-7

Now when the Sabbath was past, Mary Magdalene, Mary the mother of James, and Salome bought spices, that they might come and anoint Him (Jesus). 2 Very early in the morning, on the first day of the week, they came to the tomb when the sun had risen. 3 And they said among themselves, "Who will roll away the stone from the door of the tomb for us?" 4 But when they looked up, they saw that the stone had been rolled away—for it was very large. 5 And entering the tomb, they saw a young man clothed in a long white robe sitting on the right side; and they were alarmed. 6 But he said to them, "Do not be alarmed. You seek Jesus of Nazareth, who was crucified. He is risen! He is not here. See the place where they laid Him. 7 But go, tell His disciples—and Peter—that He is going before you into Galilee; there you will see Him, as He said to you." Mark 16:1-7

One of the issues the women thought about when they went to the tomb was about how the stone would be rolled away. More than that, there was the Roman seal on the tomb that should not be tampered with, and nobody could predict the actions from the soldiers that were guiding the tomb. Fear, worry, anxiety, panic, lack of peace of mind, emotional imbalance are some life's currencies we have to learn to give to God to handle for us. As the women got to the tomb, the first miracle was the discovery that the stone had been rolled away. Beloved, God is a difficulty-Remover! Most times, when we trust in Him, our difficulties are removed— we have to learn to lay everything on His altar as John Henry Sammis presents in his hymn:[24]

When we walk with the Lord
In the light of His word,
What a glory He sheds on our way!
While we do His good will,
He abides with us still,
And with all who will trust and obey!

Refrain:
  Trust and obey!
  For there's no other way
  To be happy in Jesus,
  But to trust and obey

But we never can prove
The delights of His love
Until all on the altar we lay;
For the favour He shows,
And the joy He bestows,
Are for those who will trust and obey.

It was obvious that the women— Mary Magdalene, Joanna, Mary the mother of James, and other women recorded in Luke 24:10, went to the tomb as mourners, but they returned as heralds of good news which assures us that turnaround is possible in the most critical situation we might find ourselves.

---

[24] John Henry Sammis, *Songs of Fellowship - Combined Words Edition,* Eastbourne: Kingsway Music, 2002, Hymn 599

Enter Your Prayer Chamber

Matthew 28:2—

> And behold, there was a great earthquake; for an angel of the Lord descended from heaven, and came and rolled back the stone from the door, and sat on it.

* The stone was an object of obstruction, hindrance and opposition, pray like this:

The power of God that sent a great earthquake from heaven during the resurrection!

— Unseat any power of Satan obstructing my life and family and set us free in the name of Jesus Christ, unseat now (repeat 7x) in the name of Jesus Christ

— Unseat any power of Satan hindering my glory and my manifestation and set me free in the mighty name of Jesus Christ, unseat now (repeat 7x) in the name of Jesus Christ

— Destroy any power of Satan impeding me and my ministry and set us free in the name of Jesus Christ, be destroyed now (repeat 7x) in the name of Jesus Christ

— Destroy any power of Satan opposing me and my business and set us free in the name of Jesus Christ

— Be destroyed now (repeat 7x) in the name of Jesus Christ.

In John 20:6-7—

> Then Simon Peter came, following him, and went into the tomb; and he saw the linen cloths lying there, 7 and the handkerchief that had been around His head, not lying with the linen cloths, but folded together in a place by itself.

* The graveclothes and the handkerchief were orderly arranged suggesting that the body of Jesus was not stolen because thieves don't have time to arrange the places they burgle. They don't waste time, they want to get away quickly. Pray like this:

Every grave and grave clothes attached to my name— catch fire! in the name of Jesus Christ. Catch fire (repeat 7x) in the name of Jesus Christ

Every grave and grave clothes programmed against me and members of my family— burn to ashes! Burn to ashes (repeat 7x) in the name of Jesus Christ

Every grave and grave clothes programmed against my Church members— burn to ashes! Burn to ashes (repeat 7x) in the name of Jesus Christ

Every grave and grave clothes reserved for any of my destiny helpers be roasted by fire! Be roasted by fire (repeat 7x) in the name of Jesus Christ

Coffin and covenant of death entered into by the wicked for my sake, backfire in the name of Jesus Christ! Backfire (repeat 7x) in the name of Jesus Christ

Coffin and covenant of death entered into by the wicked for the sake of my family, backfire in the name of Jesus Christ! Backfire (repeat 7x) in the name of Jesus Christ

Coffin and covenant of death entered into by the wicked for the sake of my Church members, backfire in the name of Jesus Christ! Backfire (repeat 7x) in the name of Jesus Christ

Coffin and covenant of death entered into by the wicked for the sake of my destiny helpers, backfire in the name of Jesus Christ!

— Backfire (repeat 7x) in the name of Jesus Christ

The news about the resurrection was a fantastic one, pray like this:

My 'resurrection news' locate me from today in the name of Jesus Christ!

My fantastic news— my life is available! Locate me now (repeat 7x) in the name of Jesus Christ

My 'resurrection news' locate me from today and let my story end well in the name of Jesus Christ

- — Let my story end well physically and spiritually
- — Let my story end well vocationally
- — Let my story end well maritally
- — Let my story end well financially
- — Let my story end well in every beneficial way in the name of Jesus Christ.

* Thank God for answering your prayers, sing songs of praise and adoration to Him, and look forward to His miracles happening in your life soonest. Remember to share the testimony of God's goodness at all times, God bless you.

APPENDIX 1

DEUTERONOMY 5:1-22

And Moses called all Israel, and said to them: "Hear, O Israel, the statutes and judgments which I speak in your hearing today, that you may learn them and be careful to observe them. 2 The LORD our God made a covenant with us in Horeb. 3 The LORD did not make this covenant with our fathers, but with us, those who are here today, all of us who are alive. 4 The LORD talked with you face to face on the mountain from the midst of the fire. 5 I stood between the LORD and you at that time, to declare to you the word of the LORD; for you were afraid because of the fire, and you did not go up the mountain. He said:

6 'I am the LORD your God who brought you out of the land of Egypt, out of the house of bondage. 7 'You shall have no other gods before Me. 8 'You shall not make for yourself a carved image—any likeness of anything that is in heaven above, or that is in the earth beneath, or that is in the water under the earth; 9 you shall not bow down to them nor serve them. For I, the LORD your God, am a jealous God, visiting the iniquity of the fathers upon the children to the third and fourth generations of those who hate Me, 10 but showing mercy to thousands, to those who love Me and keep My commandments. 11 'You shall not take the name of the LORD your God in vain, for the LORD will not hold him guiltless who takes His name in vain.

12 'Observe the Sabbath day, to keep it holy, as the LORD your God commanded you. 13 Six days you

shall labor and do all your work, 14 but the seventh day is the Sabbath of the LORD your God. In it you shall do no work: you, nor your son, nor your daughter, nor your male servant, nor your female servant, nor your ox, nor your donkey, nor any of your cattle, nor your stranger who is within your gates, that your male servant and your female servant may rest as well as you. 15 And remember that you were a slave in the land of Egypt, and the LORD your God brought you out from there by a mighty hand and by an outstretched arm; therefore the LORD your God commanded you to keep the Sabbath day. 16 'Honor your father and your mother, as the LORD your God has commanded you, that your days may be long, and that it may be well with you in the land which the LORD your God is giving you. 17 'You shall not murder. 18 'You shall not commit adultery. 19 'You shall not steal. 20 'You shall not bear false witness against your neighbor. 21 'You shall not covet your neighbor's wife; and you shall not desire your neighbor's house, his field, his male servant, his female servant, his ox, his donkey, or anything that is your neighbor's.' 22 "These words the LORD spoke to all your assembly, in the mountain from the midst of the fire, the cloud, and the thick darkness, with a loud voice; and He added no more. And He wrote them on two tablets of stone and gave them to me. Deuteronomy 5:1-22

APPENDIX 2

2 KINGS 24:1-20

Judah Overrun by Enemies

24 In his days Nebuchadnezzar king of Babylon came up, and Jehoiakim became his vassal for three years. Then he turned and rebelled against him. 2 And the LORD sent against him raiding bands of Chaldeans, bands of Syrians, bands of Moabites, and bands of the people of Ammon; He sent them against Judah to destroy it, according to the word of the LORD which He had spoken by His servants the prophets. 3 Surely at the commandment of the LORD this came upon Judah, to remove them from His sight because of the sins of Manasseh, according to all that he had done, 4 and also because of the innocent blood that he had shed; for he had filled Jerusalem with innocent blood, which the LORD would not pardon.

5 Now the rest of the acts of Jehoiakim, and all that he did, are they not written in the book of the chronicles of the kings of Judah? 6 So Jehoiakim rested with his fathers. Then Jehoiachin his son reigned in his place. 7 And the king of Egypt did not come out of his land anymore, for the king of Babylon had taken all that belonged to the king of Egypt from the Brook of Egypt to the River Euphrates.

The Reign and Captivity of Jehoiachin

8 Jehoiachin was eighteen years old when he became king, and he reigned in Jerusalem three months. His mother's name was Nehushta the daughter of Elnathan of Jerusalem. 9 And he did evil in the sight of the LORD, according to all that his father had done. 10 At that time the servants of Nebuchadnezzar king of Babylon came up against Jerusalem, and the city was besieged. 11 And Nebuchadnezzar king of Babylon came against the city, as his servants were besieging it. 12 Then Jehoiachin king of Judah, his mother, his servants, his princes, and his officers went out to the king of Babylon; and the king of Babylon, in the eighth year of his reign, took him prisoner.

The Captivity of Jerusalem

13 And he carried out from there all the treasures of the house of the LORD and the treasures of the king's house, and he cut in pieces all the articles of gold which Solomon king of Israel had made in the temple of the LORD, as the LORD had said. 14 Also he carried into captivity all Jerusalem: all the captains and all the mighty men of valor, ten thousand captives, and all the craftsmen and smiths. None remained except the poorest people of the land. 15 And he carried Jehoiachin captive to Babylon. The king's mother, the king's wives, his officers, and the mighty of the land he carried into captivity from Jerusalem to Babylon. 16 All the valiant men, seven thousand, and craftsmen and smiths, one thousand, all who were strong and fit for war, these the king of Babylon brought captive to Babylon.

Zedekiah Reigns in Judah

17 Then the king of Babylon made Mattaniah, Jehoiachin's uncle, king in his place, and changed his name to Zedekiah. 18 Zedekiah was twenty-one years old when he became king, and he reigned eleven years in Jerusalem. His mother's name was Hamutal the daughter of Jeremiah of Libnah. 19 He also did evil in the sight of the LORD, according to all that Jehoiakim had done. 20 For because of the anger of the LORD this happened in Jerusalem and Judah, that He finally cast them out from His presence. Then Zedekiah rebelled against the king of Babylon.

APPENDIX 3

2 KINGS 25:1-30

The Fall and Captivity of Judah

25 Now it came to pass in the ninth year of his reign, in the tenth month, on the tenth day of the month, that Nebuchadnezzar king of Babylon and all his army came against Jerusalem and encamped against it; and they built a siege wall against it all around. 2 So the city was besieged until the eleventh year of King Zedekiah. 3 By the ninth day of the fourth month the famine had become so severe in the city that there was no food for the people of the land. 4 Then the city wall was broken through, and all the men of war fled at night by way of the gate between two walls, which was by the king's garden, even though the Chaldeans were still encamped all around against the city. And the king went by way of the plain. 5 But the army of the Chaldeans pursued the king, and they overtook him in the plains of Jericho. All his army was scattered from him. 6 So they took the king and brought him up to the king of Babylon at Riblah, and they pronounced judgment on him. 7 Then they killed the sons of Zedekiah before his eyes, put out the eyes of Zedekiah, bound him with bronze fetters, and took him to Babylon.

8 And in the fifth month, on the seventh day of the month (which was the nineteenth year of King Nebuchadnezzar king of Babylon), Nebuzaradan the captain of the guard, a servant of the king of

Babylon, came to Jerusalem. 9 He burned the house of the LORD and the king's house; all the houses of Jerusalem, that is, all the houses of the great, he burned with fire. 10 And all the army of the Chaldeans who were with the captain of the guard broke down the walls of Jerusalem all around. 11 Then Nebuzaradan the captain of the guard carried away captive the rest of the people who remained in the city and the defectors who had deserted to the king of Babylon, with the rest of the multitude. 12 But the captain of the guard left some of the poor of the land as vinedressers and farmers. 13 The bronze pillars that were in the house of the LORD, and the carts and the bronze Sea that were in the house of the LORD, the Chaldeans broke in pieces, and carried their bronze to Babylon. 14 They also took away the pots, the shovels, the trimmers, the spoons, and all the bronze utensils with which the priests ministered. 15 The firepans and the basins, the things of solid gold and solid silver, the captain of the guard took away. 16 The two pillars, one Sea, and the carts, which Solomon had made for the house of the LORD, the bronze of all these articles was beyond measure. 17 The height of one pillar was eighteen cubits, and the capital on it was of bronze. The height of the capital was three cubits, and the network and pomegranates all around the capital were all of bronze. The second pillar was the same, with a network.

18 And the captain of the guard took Seraiah the chief priest, Zephaniah the second priest, and the three doorkeepers. 19 He also took out of the city an officer who had charge of the men of war, five men of the king's close associates who were found in the city, the chief recruiting officer of the army, who mustered the people of the land, and sixty

men of the people of the land who were found in the city. 20 So Nebuzaradan, captain of the guard, took these and brought them to the king of Babylon at Riblah. 21 Then the king of Babylon struck them and put them to death at Riblah in the land of Hamath. Thus Judah was carried away captive from its own land.

Gedaliah Made Governor of Judah

22 Then he made Gedaliah the son of Ahikam, the son of Shaphan, governor over the people who remained in the land of Judah, whom Nebuchadnezzar king of Babylon had left. 23 Now when all the captains of the armies, they and their men, heard that the king of Babylon had made Gedaliah governor, they came to Gedaliah at Mizpah—Ishmael the son of Nethaniah, Johanan the son of Careah, Seraiah the son of Tanhumeth the Netophathite, and Jaazaniah the son of a Maachathite, they and their men. 24 And Gedaliah took an oath before them and their men, and said to them, "Do not be afraid of the servants of the Chaldeans. Dwell in the land and serve the king of Babylon, and it shall be well with you." 25 But it happened in the seventh month that Ishmael the son of Nethaniah, the son of Elishama, of the royal family, came with ten men and struck and killed Gedaliah, the Jews, as well as the Chaldeans who were with him at Mizpah. 26 And all the people, small and great, and the captains of the armies, arose and went to Egypt; for they were afraid of the Chaldeans.

Jehoiachin Released from Prison

27 Now it came to pass in the thirty-seventh year of the captivity of Jehoiachin king of Judah, in the twelfth month, on the twenty-seventh day of the

month, that Evil-Merodach king of Babylon, in the year that he began to reign, released Jehoiachin king of Judah from prison. 28 He spoke kindly to him, and gave him a more prominent seat than those of the kings who were with him in Babylon. 29 So Jehoiachin changed from his prison garments, and he ate bread regularly before the king all the days of his life. 30 And as for his provisions, there was a regular ration given him by the king, a portion for each day, all the days of his life.

APPENDIX 4

JOHN 11:1-44

11 Now a certain man was sick, Lazarus of Bethany, the town of Mary and her sister Martha. 2 It was that Mary who anointed the Lord with fragrant oil and wiped His feet with her hair, whose brother Lazarus was sick. 3 Therefore the sisters sent to Him, saying, "Lord, behold, he whom You love is sick." 4 When Jesus heard that, He said, "This sickness is not unto death, but for the glory of God, that the Son of God may be glorified through it." 5 Now Jesus loved Martha and her sister and Lazarus. 6 So, when He heard that he was sick, He stayed two more days in the place where He was. 7 Then after this He said to the disciples, "Let us go to Judea again." 8 The disciples said to Him, "Rabbi, lately the Jews sought to stone You, and are You going there again?"

9 Jesus answered, "Are there not twelve hours in the day? If anyone walks in the day, he does not stumble, because he sees the light of this world. 10 But if one walks in the night, he stumbles, because the light is not in him." 11 These things He said, and after that He said to them, "Our friend Lazarus sleeps, but I go that I may wake him up." 12 Then His disciples said, "Lord, if he sleeps he will get well." 13 However, Jesus spoke of his death, but they thought that He was speaking about taking rest in sleep.14 Then Jesus said to them plainly, "Lazarus is dead. 15 And I am glad for your sakes that I was not there, that you may believe. Nevertheless let us go to him."

16 Then Thomas, who is called the Twin, said to his fellow disciples, "Let us also go, that we may die with Him."

17 So when Jesus came, He found that he had already been in the tomb four days. 18 Now Bethany was near Jerusalem, about two miles away. 19 And many of the Jews had joined the women around Martha and Mary, to comfort them concerning their brother. 20 Then Martha, as soon as she heard that Jesus was coming, went and met Him, but Mary was sitting in the house. 21 Now Martha said to Jesus, "Lord, if You had been here, my brother would not have died. 22 But even now I know that whatever You ask of God, God will give You." 23 Jesus said to her, "Your brother will rise again." 24 Martha said to Him, "I know that he will rise again in the resurrection at the last day." 25 Jesus said to her, "I am the resurrection and the life. He who believes in Me, though he may die, he shall live. 26 And whoever lives and believes in Me shall never die. Do you believe this?" 27 She said to Him, "Yes, Lord, I believe that You are the Christ, the Son of God, who is to come into the world."

28 And when she had said these things, she went her way and secretly called Mary her sister, saying, "The Teacher has come and is calling for you." 29 As soon as she heard that, she arose quickly and came to Him. 30 Now Jesus had not yet come into the town, but was in the place where Martha met Him. 31 Then the Jews who were with her in the house, and comforting her, when they saw that Mary rose up quickly and went out, followed her, saying, "She is going to the tomb to weep there." 32 Then, when Mary came where Jesus was, and saw Him, she fell down at His feet, saying to Him,

"Lord, if You had been here, my brother would not have died." 33 Therefore, when Jesus saw her weeping, and the Jews who came with her weeping, He groaned in the spirit and was troubled. 34 And He said, "Where have you laid him?" They said to Him, "Lord, come and see." 35 Jesus wept. 36 Then the Jews said, "See how He loved him!" 37 And some of them said, "Could not this Man, who opened the eyes of the blind, also have kept this man from dying?"

38 Then Jesus, again groaning in Himself, came to the tomb. It was a cave, and a stone lay against it. 39 Jesus said, "Take away the stone." Martha, the sister of him who was dead, said to Him, "Lord, by this time there is a stench, for he has been dead four days." 40 Jesus said to her, "Did I not say to you that if you would believe you would see the glory of God?" 41 Then they took away the stone from the place where the dead man was lying. And Jesus lifted up His eyes and said, "Father, I thank You that You have heard Me. 42 And I know that You always hear Me, but because of the people who are standing by I said this, that they may believe that You sent Me." 43 Now when He had said these things, He cried with a loud voice, "Lazarus, come forth!" 44 And he who had died came out bound hand and foot with graveclothes, and his face was wrapped with a cloth. Jesus said to them, "Loose him, and let him go." John 11:1-44

APPENDIX 5

BIBLICAL REFERENCES FOR OTHER HOLY SITES

Jordan: The ministry of John the Baptiser and the baptism of Jesus of Nazareth, Matthew 3:1-17; Luke 3:21-23

Mount of Temptation: Jesus left the Jordan after His baptism and was tempted for forty days, Luke 4:1-13

The Mount of Beatitudes: The entire sermon or the constitution of the Kingdom covers Matthew chapters five to seven. However, the Beatitudes (Matthew 5:1-12) presents us with the summary of the ideals required of us as citizens in Christ's kingdom.

The Storm at the Sea of Galilee: Mark 4:35-41; Matthew 8:23-27; Luke 8:22-25

At Capernaum—In the synagogue, Jesus as the bread of life, John 6:22-40, 51-66, and the healing of the paralytic: Mark 2:1-14

Pater Noster Church: This was where the disciples asked Jesus to teach them how to pray, (Our Lord's Prayer) Matthew 5:5-15

The Shepherds' Field where the angel broke the news about Jesus birth, Luke 2:1-20

Church of St. Peter in Gallicantu, Peter denied Jesus three times Matthew 26:69-75; Luke 22:54-62

En Kerem—Mary visits Elizabeth (The Church of the Visitation) Luke 1:39-55 and the birthplace of John the Baptist Luke 1:57-80

Abu Ghosh (Kiriath-Jearim), the Ark of the Lord was in the country of the Philistines, 1 Samuel 6:1-21; 7:1-2, 2 Samuel 6:1-15

BOOKS BY THE AUTHOR

101 REASONS WHY PEOPLE FAIL IN LEADERSHIP

THE AMBASSADOR'S MIRROR

FORGIVE & FORGET — GOD'S LOVE TOWARDS MANKIND

THE NATURE OF GRACE — REDEMPTION FOR
UNDESERVING HUMANITY BEYOND NOAHIC TIME

PRAYER RAIN — AN ESSENTIAL MASTER-KEY FOR
CHRISTIAN PILGRIMS FOR RETREAT & THE HOLY LAND

BIBLIOGRAPHY

Archer, G. L., Contribution on Isaiah in Charles F. Pfeiffer, (ed.,), *The Wycliffe Bible Commentary*, (Chicago: Moody Press, 1962)

France, R. T., Commentary on Matthew, in Leon Morris, (General ed.,), *Tyndale New Testament Commentaries,* (Leicester, England: Inter-Varsity Press, 1985)

Guthrie, D., Contribution on John, The Pastoral Letters in D. A Carson, et al, (Consulting eds), *New Bible Commentary, 21st Century Edition*, (Leicester, England: Inter-Varsity Press, 1994)

Hickey, M., *The Gospel of John - Classic Library Edition*, (Denver, Colorado: Marilyn Hickey Ministries, 2000)

Jamieson, R., Fausset, A. R., Brown, D., *Commentary On The Whole Bible*, (Grand Rapids, Michigan: Zondervan Publishing House, 1961)

MacDonald, W., (Art Farstad ed.), *Believer's Bible Commentary — A Complete Bible Commentary in One Volume*, (London: Thomas Nelson Publishers, 1995)

Matthew Henry's Commentary on The Whole Bible, (Chicago, Illinois: Operation Mobilization Literature, 1995)

Morris, L., (General ed.,), *Luke - Tyndale New Testament Commentaries,* (Leicester, England: Inter-Varsity Press, 1999)

Motyer, A., Contribution on The Psalms, Amos in D. A Carson, et al (Consulting eds.,), *New Bible Commentary, 21st Century Edition*, (Leicester, England: Inter-Varsity Press, 1994)

Tasker, R. V. G., (General ed.,), *John, Tyndale New Testament Commentaries,* (Leicester, England: Inter-Varsity Press, 1999)

Unger, M. F., *Unger Bible Handbook, An Essential Guide to Understanding the Bible,* (Chicago: Moody Press, 1967)

Bibles
New King James Version

Scripture taken from the New King James Version®.

Copyright © 1982 by Thomas Nelson. Used by Permission. All rights reserved.

The Living Bible

Life Application Bible, Verses marked TLB are taken from The Living Bible copyright © 1971. Used by permission of Tyndale House Publishers, Inc., Wheaton, Illinois 60189. All rights reserved.

Hymn

Compilation of Songs & Hymns, *Songs of Fellowship - Combined Words Edition,* Eastbourne: Kingsway Music, 2002

Websites

Article by Menachem Posner in Chabad.org (chabad.org/library/article_cdo/aid/5115389/jewish/9-facts-You-Should-Know-About-Mount-Sinai.htm). Cited on 16/07/2023

https://www.biblegateway.com

www.ingramcontent.com/pod-product-compliance
Lightning Source LLC
Chambersburg PA
CBHW051830040426

42447CB00006B/449